Prince Eugene, the

L. Würdig

Alpha Editions

This edition published in 2024

ISBN 9789362095466

Design and Setting By
Alpha Editions
www.alphaedis.com
Email - info@alphaedis.com

As per information held with us this book is in Public Domain.
This book is a reproduction of an important historical work.
Alpha Editions uses the best technology to reproduce historical work
in the same manner it was first published to preserve its original nature.
Any marks or number seen are left intentionally to preserve.

Contents

Translator's Preface .... - 1 -

Prologue .... - 2 -

Chapter I   The Little Capuchin .... - 3 -

Chapter II   The Siege of Vienna .... - 11 -

Chapter III   Turkish Campaigns .... - 16 -

Chapter IV   The Battle of Zenta .... - 21 -

Chapter V   War of the Spanish Succession .... - 26 -

Chapter VI   Blenheim .... - 37 -

Chapter VII   The Italian Campaign .... - 44 -

Chapter VIII   Malplaquet .... - 48 -

Chapter IX   Eugene at Belgrade .... - 56 -

Chapter X   Last Days .... - 64 -

Footnotes .... - 71 -

Translator's Preface

The story of the brilliant career of Eugene, generally known as Prince Eugene of Savoy, has its special lesson for youth. He was intended for the Church, but was ambitious for a military career. Louis the Fourteenth had marked out for him the profession of an *abbé*; but monarchs, even the most powerful, do not always dispose. When "the little Capuchin," as he was contemptuously called, applied to that sovereign for a commission in the French army and was refused it, he shook the French dust from his feet and went to Austria, resolved that France some day should suffer for that refusal. The story shows how his resolution was carried out. The Austrian Emperor gladly welcomed him. He rose from a subordinate position in the army to become one of the greatest generals of his time. All Europe felt the strength of the "little Capuchin's" arm. He was a born soldier and war was the passion of his life. His career, seems almost like an inspiration. He won battles, often against largely superior forces, by the rapidity and dash of his attacks, by a personal courage which never wavered, and by a magnetic influence which inspired the admiration of his own soldiers and fear among his enemies. He was in the field more than fifty years. The ten peaceful years of his life were devoted to literature and the arts; but the battle-field was the scene of his life's success. The story which his life has for youth is the result which may be accomplished, not merely on battle-fields, but in every department of action, by determined purpose, resolute will, and tireless industry. The "little Capuchin" spurned the ease and comfort and luxury of an *abbé* for the rough fare of the soldier, and made himself the foremost general of his time by the exercise of these qualities.

G. P. U.

CHICAGO, *July, 1910.*

Prologue

Prince Eugene, the great warrior and statesman, although scion of an Italian family, and by birth a Frenchman, became a thorough German. He appeared at a critical time in the relations between Germany and France, to save his adopted fatherland from destruction, and to illuminate the darkest period of German history with the glory of a series of the most splendid and heroic achievements. The historian Von Sybel calls him "the greatest general and statesman of Austria." As a statesman he overtops the greatest of his successors, Kaunitz and Stadion. As a general he fills a place, chronologically and in rank, just between Gustavus Adolphus and Frederick the Great. He was a dashing hero and at the same time possessed a sympathetic nature. He was a genial companion, a conscientious patriot, a master in politics, and an upright man. Wherever he appeared he charmed. Although a born Frenchman of Italian stock, he showed truer German feeling and spirit than most of the Austrian leaders. He was one of those characters whom any nation might be proud to possess. He served the Austrian imperial house for fifty-three years, thereby contributing to the glory of the country.

Chapter I
The Little Capuchin

Prince Eugene of Savoy-Carignan, the hero of this story, takes foremost rank among the greatest generals and statesmen of all times. This strange French-sounding name may seem odd for a German hero; but in this case it is quite misleading, for no one ever had deeper German sympathies; no German soldier ever hated the people on the banks of the Seine more bitterly. He gave them plenty of hard blows, and has been christened by the German people—and not without reason—"Prince Eugene, the chivalrous knight."

Prince Eugene was born in Paris, although his ancestral land was Savoy, the well-known duchy, formerly part of upper Italy, a barren mountainous country. He first saw the light in the capital city of that country which was afterwards to suffer so cruelly by his mailed hand. The ways of Providence often seem strange, as in this instance, when in the heart of France the man was born who was to teach France and the Frenchmen respect for the Germans. France had ever been arrogant toward Germany, and was particularly so at that time and until, in 1813-14-15 and later in 1870 and 1871, she was taught a wholesome lesson.

And now I must tell you how Prince Eugene came to be born in Paris. In the first half of the seventeenth century Prince Thomas Francis of Savoy, youngest son of the reigning Duke Charles Emanuel the First, founded the collateral line of the house of Savoy-Carignan. His wife was Marie of Bourbon, sister and heiress of the last Count of Soissons; his two sons, Emanuel Philibert and Eugene Maurice. The latter took the title of Count of Soissons and married Olympia Mancini, a niece of the notorious French minister, Mazarin. From this marriage sprang three daughters and five sons, of whom Prince Eugene was the youngest.

History tells us that Prince Eugene's father was a man of gracious manners and of a brave and genial disposition. He distinguished himself in feats of arms, and was therefore a favorite at the court of King Louis the Fourteenth of France. Eugene's mother was a beautiful woman and very fond of the gay life of the time; to her all the homage was rendered that feminine beauty and wit were wont to receive at the brilliant court of "His Most Christian Majesty."[1]

The palace of Count Eugene Maurice of Soissons was situated upon the site where the great Grain Market of Paris now stands. If one of my readers should happen to visit that city he may look upon the spot and meditate upon the instability of all earthly things.[2] This palace had a long, memorable, and brilliant history. In the fourteenth century it was the property of King John of Bohemia, of the house of Luxembourg; it next served as the cloister of a sect of expiatory nuns and later passed into the hands of the notorious Catherine de Medici, who furnished it in all the extravagant taste of the time. It stood in the midst of splendid gardens, embellished with fountains and colonnades; and in the interior of the park was a chapel of truly royal magnificence. It may be, that in this sacred spot Catherine de Medici, mother of that monster, Charles IX, may have conceived the idea, for the advancement and honor of her church, of the Paris massacre. It was in this palace that Eugene was born, October 18, 1663, one hundred and fifty years before the great battle of Leipzig, a victory which broke the power of the first Napoleon over Germany. This date, which the year 1813 made a memorable one for Germany, would seem more suitably marked in our calendars by the name of "Eugene" or "Lebrecht" rather than by that of some saint.

Before we concern ourselves with Eugene or his parents, let us finish the history of the palace of Soissons. For almost a century it remained in the hands of the family. Then a dishonest Scot by the name of Law founded a bank in Paris, which soon became bankrupt, beggaring many thousands of the well-to-do citizens. At last the city of Paris bought the ill-fated building in order to erect on the site of so much crime and sin, wild lust and miserable treachery, a very practical building, the above-mentioned Grain Market, thereby to wipe out the dark past.

Eugene's cradle stood in the midst of gay and luxurious surroundings. The palace of Soissons was the resort of the flower of the French nobility. Brilliant *fêtes*, in which the King never failed to be among the guests, followed one another, and the youthful mistress, the beautiful Italian, Olympia Mancini, was the flower of them all. At last the magnet lost its power, as it is ever prone to do where court life is subject to the moods and caprices of a tyrannical ruler. Intrigues were set on foot against the Count and Countess of Soissons; their powerful relative, the minister Mazarin, had long been dead, and both of them were banished from the court by a royal decree dated March 30, 1665, and ordered to their country estates. One can imagine the feelings of Olympia particularly, who had been the petted favorite and ornament of the royal court for years. She shed no vain tears over her fate, however, but cherished in her heart a thirst for revenge. She now hated with a deadly hatred the King whom she had loved and honored, and this sentiment she inculcated in her children. This seed, hatred of the house of Bourbon and particularly of the King, fell in good soil. Her son Eugene preserved this heritage from his mother throughout his whole life.

Eugene was ten years old when his father suddenly died. After this blow, fortune seemed utterly to forsake the Countess. In order to retrieve it, she was ready to seize on any means, even the most unworthy. She studied astrology and fortune telling, and in this way became associated with a person named Voisin, who was finally prosecuted as a poisoner. Just in time Olympia, learning that she was to be arrested as an accomplice, fled to Flanders. But even abroad, in Brussels, she was pursued by the hatred of her former friends. It was Louis's minister Louvois particularly who heaped insults upon her.

For the honor of Eugene's mother, the Countess of Soissons, it must be said that the totally unfounded rumors against her were at last silenced. Not a trace of complicity with the crime of the Voisin woman has been discovered. The talented Countess soon made many influential friends in Brussels. Her salon became very popular, and these social triumphs somewhat compensated for the wrongs suffered in Paris.

At the time of her flight the Countess had left her children with the mother of her deceased husband, the Princess of Carignan. Their grandmother sought to give them a good education and to provide for their future. Four of her grandsons were already in the army, three in France, and one, Julius, in the German imperial service; but she had difficulties with Eugene, the fifth and youngest. In short, Eugene was intended for the priesthood, but was determined to become a soldier instead. Of princely birth, as a member of the clergy, his future would have been secure; in time he might have enjoyed fat revenues, and sometime and somewhere have occupied a bishop's seat. This goal might have tempted many of his rank, but it was not so with him. He might also have entered into service at court and would probably have prospered outwardly there, but with his nature and talents how unhappy he would have been if thus misplaced! The mere thought of becoming a courtier and toady of his French majesty, the "Most Christian King," who was as bigoted as he was godless, treacherous, and unjust; who had driven Eugene's parents into banishment and had heaped unjust suspicion, insult, and injury upon his mother, was repugnant to him.

He was firmly resolved to become a soldier. In his earliest youth he had shown a pronounced, even unconquerable predilection for the profession, and had concentrated all his dreams and hopes and his whole education upon it. Mathematics had always been his favorite study. With resolute purpose he had applied himself to the study of geometry under a friend of Vauban, the great French master of fortifications, whose excellent buildings, walls, moats, redoubts, lunettes, and bastions caused German soldiers trouble enough, even in the last war. His favorite book was the life of Alexander, the great King of Macedonia, by Curtius; his principal models were Hannibal and Cæsar. He would pore over every work on battles and sieges he could find, and his eyes glistened when he heard the clashing of weapons. Possessing such tastes and talents, there was but one insuperable obstacle to his becoming a soldier: he was of a very delicate physique and had been sickly in his early years. Although he persistently exercised and took every means to harden and toughen himself, his nature could not be altered, and to his great chagrin he remained small and delicate even when he had reached maturity.

"I shall be a soldier for all that," he often said with great determination to those who good naturedly meant to discourage him, and then he would add: "but no carpet-knight or soldier on parade, like those who guard the Louvre day and night that His Majesty may sleep soundly, and who swagger about in gold and silver braid, conniving at the adventures of the princes and royal family. No! I wish to be a real soldier; one who is ready in the face of any hardship to do his sworn duty to the death."

Here his good grandmother of the house of Bourbon probably smiled and shook her finger in warning; and no doubt her grandson answered her: "If it be God's will, you shall yet see me a field-marshal at the head of an army."

It was useless to gainsay such a spirit as this. Eugene had a head of his own, as they say, and had quietly made up his mind to let time solve the problem. There was still another difficulty and a very serious one. The will of the King had destined the little fatherless boy, whom circumstances had also deprived of a mother's guidance, for the Church instead of the army. It is very likely that he thought that such an obstinate little princeling of the house of Savoy should not be allowed to have his own way, but must be taught to obey.

We shall see what came to pass. Of course it was impossible to contend with a Louis the Fourteenth, for he had plenty of means for compelling obedience. He had long ago made up his mind to break this youthful obstinacy and prevent Eugene from entering the French army. At last came the time when Eugene must decide. Through good friends he had several times tried to sound the King's disposition in the matter, and always with discouraging results. Eugene, whom the King sarcastically called "the little *abbé*" said to himself: "You must be a man, and if you ever intend to march at the head of an army and confront an enemy armed to the teeth, you cannot afford to be afraid of the King of France! So there!"

One fine day Eugene begged for an audience, which was granted. At last he stood before His Majesty, King Louis the Fourteenth, whom his creatures called "The Great." Eugene and Louis! One cannot imagine two natures more unlike in every respect, inwardly and outwardly. One elevated Germany to a position of honor and power; the other would have been glad to drag it down in order to be worshipped as its ruler. Standing erect, with clear and honest eyes, in a resolute voice, Eugene presented to the King his petition for a commission in the army.

When he had finished, the King's eyes rested upon him for some moments with an expression of derision. The "little *abbé*" had never before seemed so repulsive to him. Eugene certainly was far from being a paragon of beauty. His complexion was dark, he was small in stature, and his nose was comparatively large. His upper lip was so short that his mouth remained constantly open, disclosing the front teeth. The redeeming feature was his eyes which, intelligent and fiery, gazed intently at the King as though they would read his fate from his lips.

"You are disobedient, *abbé*," said the King in a cutting voice; "you oppose my will."

"Not your will, Your Majesty," answered Eugene, "but only an office for which I have no inclination."

"But you are not fit for a soldier," said the King, measuring him from head to foot with an almost disdainful look. "You will never be able to bear the hardships of the service. As I happen to know, your father had destined you for the priesthood. Take back your petition."

"All my ancestors have followed the profession of arms," answered Eugene; "it is the most honorable one for a prince, it is——"

"Silence with your arguments," interrupted the King; "I am in no mood to listen to them. You know my wish. I will suffer no contradiction. A prince of Savoy-Carignan should——" Here the King cleared his throat and could not at once find the right expression for what he wished to say.

PRINCE EUGENE
before King Louis the Fourteenth

"Should," Eugene took up the unfinished remark, "should at least have the liberty of deciding his own future and of choosing his profession."

"The little *abbé* is excited," said the King in a disdainful tone. Then he continued, "It shall be as I have commanded. Your Reverence must enter into holy orders very shortly."

"Your Majesty," replied Eugene with a firmness of voice and manner far beyond his years (for he was then only seventeen), "you force me to declare that I shall embrace the profession of arms in spite of everything."

"But not under my flag, not in France," cried the King forbiddingly.

"Then I am compelled to seek another sovereign and another fatherland."

"Do so, Prince. You are dismissed."

Eugene immediately obeyed this command. His future was decided.

"This person's face is very repulsive to me," said the King to his courtiers. "The Soissons were all pig-headed and this fellow has inherited his mother's audacious spirit besides. Louvois is right, all these Soissons must learn to submit."

So thought the King. But man proposes; God disposes. This Soissons (Eugene) at least did not feel the power of the King of France; the reverse was the case, which we shall see as our history proceeds. The heart of Prince Eugene was light as a feather when he had turned his back upon the King and his grand palace. Now all was clear between them; he had spoken his mind and told the King the truth, as he had probably never heard it spoken before by one of his vassals.

When one considers, it was certainly a very daring procedure. Abruptly and quickly he had broken all the ties that bound him to the King and his house. It was certainly not a bad thing to have the powerful King of France for a cousin. Had Eugene, according to the King's demand, become a priest, he would have fared well, might have folded his hands on his knees and have enjoyed a very comfortable living. But now it was necessary to stand on his own feet and to act with hands and brain. Thousands would certainly have decided differently, would have preferred the certain to the uncertain and have considered that a piece of bread in the mouth is better than a feather in the cap.

Eugene did not belong to this order of mankind. Fate had early taken him in hand. His father's cares and his mother's tears had sunk deeply into his heart. He was too good a son to forget easily the wrongs inflicted by the King. He had also been early introduced to the frivolous life at court, and had conceived a disgust for it. Thirdly and lastly, he had a lively faith in God. He believed firmly in an all-wise heavenly control of the universe, had put his trust in the King of kings, and was at peace with himself. He would never have been a successful priest, but he was enthusiastic for the profession of arms.

The next problem for Eugene to solve was, under whom he should seek service. France was not the world. There were many potentates under whose banners he could find honor and fame. He hesitated but a short time; then his intuition came to his aid and he chose the German Emperor. Strangely enough, although a Frenchman by birth, his heart had always turned to Germany; from youth German deeds of valor had inspired him. Added to this, his uncle, the Duke of Savoy, was on the most friendly terms with the Emperor Leopold the First, and his brother Julius, who had entered the imperial service shortly before, had already been assigned to the command of a regiment.

Eugene lost no time. He said farewell to his grandmother and to his brothers and sisters, and packed his belongings. These, no doubt, were not numerous, for his pleasure-loving mother had attended to that; and besides, the parental legacy had been widely distributed. But this troubled Eugene very little. In eating, in drinking, and in dress he was accustomed to the greatest simplicity; and in case of need he had a rich uncle in Savoy, who would have considered it a disgrace, as he had a great deal of family pride, to let his young relative suffer want.

Accompanied by a single servant, Eugene left Paris and shook the dust of the proud capital from his feet. It is said that he vowed never to enter France again except as her enemy, sword in hand, at the head of a German army. We shall see later how this came to pass. And now let us heartily wish good luck to our determined young Savoyard.

Chapter II
The Siege of Vienna

Eugene arrived at last in Vienna, although the journey then consumed much longer time than it does to-day. This had its advantages, for one had time to consider one's plans and to make up one's mind whether one were doing the right thing or not. But, as we already know, Eugene was not the man to vacillate when once he had decided. When he had the goal before him he made straight for it, looking neither to right nor left; in fine, he no doubt felt that God was leading him; and this is the best guide for us all, whether prince or beggar.

At the royal castle in Vienna he was very kindly received. He had not grown handsomer or statelier on the road from Paris to Vienna; but Emperor Leopold overlooked these externals and saw something deeper. Eugene's firmness of bearing, his directness of speech, and his whole personality impressed him. There were other considerations also which influenced the Emperor. Like Eugene, he had been destined in youth for the Church; he was also pleased to have princes and cousins of the already powerful Duke of Savoy, flocking to his banner at a time when the operations of the rapacious and murderous Turk were becoming more and more of a menace to Vienna. Every German sword that freely offered itself was welcomed as a real acquisition. So thought the Emperor. To be sure the Viennese had other ideas, for with all their amiability they have a sense of humor.

The little Prince of Savoy-Carignan was almost too tiny for them. When they had heard his story, they scarcely blamed the French King for having destined this little chap for the priesthood. They insisted that he was not fit for war. They called him "The little Capuchin"—a name which fitted him, for he generally wore a long brown cloak which closely resembled a monk's habit. Very often people stopped on the streets, shaking their heads, to gaze after him. Eugene would have had to be very obtuse not to have noticed this. At present it could not be helped, but he no doubt thought to himself, "Just wait, and sooner or later the little Capuchin will show you what he can do." There was that within him which neither the edicts of a king of France nor the jokes of the Viennese could subdue; genius was bound to assert itself. His opportunity soon came.

The Turks as well as the French were enemies of the empire at that time. Until quite recent times the German people were accustomed, in their church prayers, to call on God for protection against both these enemies. The French were constantly harassing the empire on its western frontier, and the Turks on the eastern. Here and there great domains were taken, and it is only to be wondered at that under such desperate circumstances it did not go quite to pieces. This shows how full of tenacity and endurance the German people were. The worst of the situation at that time was that "the Most Christian" King of France encouraged the Turks and was playing the game with them. He argued that if the Germans were busy in Vienna with the Turks, the Emperor could not send an army to the Rhine; and the beautiful country on both sides of this river had long excited his cupidity. Shortly before this (1681) Strasburg had fallen into his hands through abominable treachery. Such a rich morsel had excited Louis the Fourteenth's appetite anew.

In Hungary, which was the portal of entry into the empire for the Turks, the ruler was an adventurous spirit and a dare-devil soldier, named Tökely, who had been bribed by Louis. Indeed, as many historians tell us, he had a secret understanding with the Turks for the destruction of Germany. It was very difficult to accomplish this from the French side, for here a stanch German prince opposed him and defended German rights against the impious attacks of the French. This German prince was Frederick William, the great elector of Brandenburg. You see it was even then one of the Hohenzollerns who entered the lists in Germany's behalf; how long they have been misunderstood and accused of base schemes of conquest!

But let us pass from the Hohenzollerns to the French, Hungarians, and Turks. The Emperor had concluded a twenty-years' armistice with the last of these after the battle of St. Gotthard. This was now nearly at an end. If the court of Vienna had made good use of it, the Turks never would have dared to attack this still powerful enemy. As it was, they had been sitting with folded hands, idle and impassive. The imperial army was small in numbers and insufficiently fitted out. The fortresses in Hungary were in a neglected condition, and the country itself was kept in disorder and insurrection by Tökely and his lawless followers. Thus it was an easy matter for the Turks to subdue not only Hungary but other sections of Austria, and to carry the victorious crescent to the very gates of Vienna.

It was during this period of nervous anxiety that, by imperial command, Prince Eugene was given a lieutenant's commission in the dragoon regiment of his brother, Prince Julius Louis of Savoy-Carignan, in order that he might win his spurs under the latter's eye. The commander of the imperial army was Duke Charles of Lorraine, who had a tale to tell of the French King's arrogance, as he also had been spurned in that country. What must have been Prince Eugene's feelings when he first donned the imperial uniform! His entry into the Austrian army gives us much food for thought. His future had not been foretold from the cradle; but who knows what would have become of the German fatherland had he gone to Spain instead of to Austria; had he never striven against the Turks; if in the Spanish war of succession he had fought against instead of for Germany; if the French instead of being his enemies had been his friends?

Instantly the torch of war was ablaze. The Turks and Hungarians, uniting, pushed forward from the lower Danube. Burning villages and towns, desolated landscapes, hunger, misery, and all the horrors of war marked their path. Many thousands of youths and maidens fell into their hands, to be carried away as hostages or to be sold into slavery. All was confusion, and no one could suggest a remedy. The whole Austrian army numbered 35,000 men, and the Turks were 200,000 strong. What a contrast!

The operations of the Emperor's troops were mostly unsuccessful. They were anxious to hinder the enemy's advance, so that the Viennese might have time to strengthen their intrenchments. Perceiving this, the Grand Vizier pushed rapidly forward to the Leitha; and in order not to be cut off from Vienna, Duke Charles of Lorraine was obliged to change his position. He was attacked with furious impetuosity at Petronell, July 7, 1683, by the advance-guard of the Turkish army. It was a bloody engagement, for it was necessary for the Germans to defend themselves at any cost.

It was there that Eugene met the enemy for the first time and proved himself a soldier. He fought as bravely as the best, keeping at his brother's side, wherever the danger was greatest. The King of France should have seen the little *abbé* in this wild cavalry encounter—he would certainly have changed his mind. Despite their ardor the Turks were obliged to retire, and this pleased Eugene mightily. But unfortunately the joy of victory was embittered by a great sorrow. His beloved brother Julius was a victim of the day's work and was found, terribly disfigured, under the horses' hoofs. Eugene shed some bitter tears, said a prayer for his brother's soul, then pressed on after the enemy.

But it was impossible to stem the tide of their superior numbers; already they had surrounded Vienna, and a division of Turkish cavalry had taken possession of one of the suburbs, where they were conducting themselves in truly barbaric style. That could not be tolerated. The Margrave, Louis of Baden, who had succeeded Prince Julius Louis of Soissons as commander of the dragoon regiment, attacked the Turks, sabre in hand, cut down many of them and put the rest to flight. Eugene took part in this fight with enthusiasm; as also a few days later at Presburg, where the Duke of Lorraine defeated the rear-guard of the enemy. Here also the dragoons of the Margrave Louis of Baden did their part, and Eugene distinguished himself above all the rest.

In the meantime the main army of the Turks, under command of the Grand Vizier, Kora Mustapha, had entirely surrounded Vienna. Such peril had never before befallen a German city. All Germany was in a fever of excitement. It was plain that, should Vienna fall, the whole German empire would be open to the marauding and murdering infidels; and God knows what might come next. But it turned out differently. The mayor of Vienna, Rudiger von Starhemberg, was a good soldier as well as administrator. Here he encouraged, there led an attack; and the Viennese citizens and students fought like heroes under his leadership. Although the Turks stormed the walls and had even made a breach here and there, they were obliged to retreat before the defenders, who were fighting for their dearest and most sacred possessions. The good Viennese, however, would have been obliged at last to succumb, had not help come from the Electors of Bavaria and Saxony, the Emperor's troops under Duke Charles of Lorraine, and with them, of course, the chief of the dragoon regiment, Margrave Louis of Baden, with "the little Capuchin," Prince Eugene, all led by King John Sobieski of Poland. The Capuchin was already become a mighty hero; Eugene had smelled powder, and even the dragoons, who had at first regarded him doubtfully, had quite changed their minds about him.

The decisive battle took place September 12, 1683, under the walls of Vienna. The assistance was timely, for the city could scarce have held out twenty-four hours longer. The Turks had been bombarding it since the fifteenth of July. It was a wonder that it had resisted so long. The last day was destined to be the hardest one for the Viennese. The Grand Vizier had divided his army. Legions attacked the deliverers on the Kalenberg, and other legions were commanded to take the city. For a long time the outcome was uncertain. The Turks fought with incomparable ferocity and recklessness; and it became necessary for the Germans to exert their strength to the utmost against their attacks. The fury and confusion were terrible, the slaughter unparalleled. Wild cries to Allah mingled with the groans and prayers of the Christians. Blood flowed in streams, and the trenches were filled with the corpses of friend and foe alike. It was well that the decisive moment was at hand, for the defenders had expended their last effort. At length the trumpeters sounded the glad tidings of victory from the Cathedral tower of St. Stephen, from whence the flight of the Turks could be seen. It was heroic work, in which every man did his share, and especially Prince Eugene. With the Duke of Lorraine, he pushed down the steep declivity of Leopoldsberg toward Nussdorf, then along the banks of the Danube, in pursuit of the enemy.

Once more the Turks made a sharp and ferocious attack on the walls and intrenchments of Vienna. Although repulsed on the outside, they were determined to take the city. The danger increased, but little more patience and endurance was needed, for help was at hand. Margrave Louis of Baden detected the greatest danger-point at the Schottenthor (Scotch Gate). With three battalions of infantry and his dragoon regiment he cut his way to this point. He wished to outflank the enemy and give the Viennese a breathing spell. Prince Eugene was at every point where the danger was greatest. With his dragoons he was the first to enter the Scotch Gate. What a slashing and butchering there was! It was necessary to effect a meeting with Starhemberg. The long blades of the dragoons did terrific execution among the enemy. At the head stormed the "little Capuchin," giving orders here and striking a blow there, until he heard trumpet calls from the other side. It was Starhemberg, and the Turks were between two fires; there was no longer any escape, they must go down in this sea of fire and flame.

Vienna was saved. The Turks fled, and the dragoons kept close at their heels. Order had now to be restored in all directions.

A little defeat which the Polish cavalry had suffered on the seventh of October at Parkan was revenged two days later by the reunited army. Margrave Louis of Baden took the city by storm; then Gran surrendered, and this closed the famous campaign of the year 1683.

Before the year had closed Prince Eugene had received the thanks of the Emperor for his gallantry. On the twelfth of December, 1683, he was appointed Commander and Colonel of the Kuefstein regiment of dragoons; and this fine regiment he retained without a break during his long career. For a long time it had the honor of being a model for the whole imperial cavalry. And is it a wonder? Prince Eugene understood his profession and was a past master in the art of war.

Chapter III
Turkish Campaigns

Although there were no telegraph stations at that time nor any railroads, it soon became known in Versailles and Paris that the "little abbé" had fought very gallantly, and that his bravery had received recognition from the Emperor. What must Louis have felt when he heard this news? He was too crafty to betray himself; but Louvois was less self-contained, and cried in his wrath: "This fellow shall never again enter France." It was easy for this presumptuous minister to issue his commands, but the fulfilment of his purpose was not in his power. Eugene had now gained an assured position. His commanding officer, the Field-Marshal General, Margrave Louis of Baden, a man for those times very well informed and an accomplished soldier, possessed far more discrimination than the King of France displayed in that memorable audience at the Louvre; he recommended Eugene to the Emperor with the words: "In time this young Savoyard will be the equal of all those whom the world considers great generals."

The campaign of 1684 was quickly opened, but without particular success. It is a long distance from Vienna to Stamboul, and there was much to be done before the enemy could be despatched thither. They still had their strongholds in Hungary, and such neighbors were dangerous. It was necessary above all to seize Buda.[3] At first this was unsuccessful; indeed, the Germans were obliged to go into winter quarters without having accomplished anything; then they had to put the city in a state of siege and to resist the advance of the Turkish army of relief. Starhemberg proposed to take Neuhäusel first, this being the only way to approach Buda. The good advice of this experienced soldier was disregarded, and therefore unfortunate consequences had to be endured. It was not until the next year that the situation improved. Other powers had gathered their forces under the banners of the Austrian Emperor, including Bavaria, Saxony, Brandenburg and twenty thousand Hungarians who were opposed to Tökely and chose to adhere to the Emperor rather than to this impostor.

Since the siege of Vienna, by the enemies of Christianity, there had been an awakening among the German princes; the common danger had called for common defence. Of course Prince Eugene with his regiment was not wanting. His post was on the left wing of the imperial cavalry commanded by the Prince Salm. Everything prospered so that Buda was soon as completely surrounded as Vienna had previously been by the Turks.

Eugene, with his dragoons, held a ravine road on the south side of the fortress, which led between two mountains into a broad plain. From this quarter the Turks in Buda were expecting their relief forces; and nearly every day there were skirmishes, in which, however, the Turks always got the worst of it. How dangerous these engagements were, is shown by the fact that once Prince Eugene's horse was shot under him, and another time he was wounded by an arrow.

The Turkish supporting army at last arrived, but was completely vanquished, and the city was then taken by storm. Eugene very nearly missed this fun, for he was on sentry duty and was commanded to remain at his post. But when he heard the thunder of the field-pieces, great and small, the clash of swords and the sound of the trumpets, he could no longer contain himself. He quickly ordered a part of his dragoons to mount, battered down a gate with axes, and in a moment was in the thick of the fray beside his victorious German brothers.

Now began the second rout. Valiant Eugene had the honor of chasing the enemy over the Danube. Ha! that was merry work! Besides this, Fünfkirchen was taken by Eugene's unmounted dragoons. Once started, he would have done still more, had not a very deplorable misunderstanding and jealousy among the Emperor's commanders stopped all important operations for some time to come. None wished to obey another. Margrave Louis of Baden dared to tell the Duke of Lorraine to his face, that he was not obliged, as a German Prince, to take orders from him. The young Elector of Bavaria, Maximilian Emanuel, also made trouble.

This was a great disadvantage to the Germans, and grieved Eugene deeply. The situation did not improve until the Turks became more and more menacing, and this danger brought the malcontents to their senses. At last, on the twelfth of August, 1687, it was determined to attack the Turks at Mohacz.

Here, almost on the same spot where, one hundred and sixty years earlier, King Louis the Second of Hungary had lost empire and life to Suleyman, he was at last avenged. The battle lasted only a short time, but the victory was a decisive one. Like a wall of brass the Germans slowly advanced. There was no break of which their opponents could take advantage. The attacks of the enemy's cavalry broke against it, like the breaking of the sea against the rocks. Again and again the Turks attacked, and were driven back each time. Added to this, a steady fire of musketry raked their lines, and the cannon did their duty also. At last there was no possibility of restraining the soldiers; and the time had come, too, for Eugene to let loose his dragoons. Like a whirlwind they threw themselves on the Turks, whole regiments were ridden down and others taken prisoners. Once more the Turks made a stand behind their intrenchments; they thought Eugene could not get at them there. But how mistaken they were! Like lightning his dragoons were off their horses, drew their sabres, stormed the barricades, and cut down all who did not save themselves by instant flight.

Thus the battle was decided; the lion's share of the victory and of the glory was Eugene's. This, no doubt, was appreciated by the Duke of Lorraine; for as a reward for his daring dash at Mohacz, he sent him in person to bear the news of victory to Vienna. It was certainly a proud commission for the valiant Prince! Arrived at the castle, he instantly received audience and was presented by the Emperor with his portrait richly set in diamonds.

After the battle of Mohacz Eugene's fame was assured, his name was on every tongue. The king of Spain bestowed upon him the Order of the Golden Fleece; and his cousin, the reigning Duke of Savoy, Victor Amadeus the First, delighted with the brilliant success of his young relative, supplied him royally with money.

How the gentlemen in Paris and Versailles must have opened their eyes at all this! Their historical works, as one can well believe, do not tell of any distinction that Eugene received. King Louis must have been thoroughly ashamed of his shortsightedness; he had taken the rough diamond for a common pebble. Prince Eugene became Lieutenant-Field-Marshal in his twenty-fifth year. This was certainly an unusual distinction. What is more important, he became Lieutenant-Field-Marshal not through the favor of the king, but on his own merits.

It was now most important for the Emperor to regain possession of Belgrade. The last bulwark of the Germans could not be allowed to remain in the hands of the Turks. The Emperor commanded; there was no hesitation. The Elector of Bavaria, the Emperor's son-in-law, was now commander of the imperial army after the valiant Duke Charles of Lorraine had been diplomatically removed.

The affair went splendidly. When the German cannon had shot but two breaches in the walls, the assault was made. Two columns advanced to the fortifications, led by the Elector and Eugene. The cry was: "Long live the Emperor; long live Germany!" They advanced quite a long distance and thought they had already won the day. But they were mistaken; for a deep moat protected the real fort and made a dangerous obstacle. There was little time to consider; it was do—or die! In spite of the continuous fire of the Turks, young Count Starhemberg, nephew of the heroic Vienna Mayor, called out: "Follow me, he who loves the Emperor and his country!" He then sprang into the moat up to his belt, his whole regiment following him. But this was by no means the end. As they climbed out of the moat, dripping wet, they had to take the intrenchments. The Turks defended themselves desperately, for they knew what it meant to lose Belgrade. But the Elector and Eugene followed hard upon the heels of the Starhemberg regiment. There was a terrible hand-to-hand fight, while large and small missiles fell right and left among the attacking army. The Elector received an arrow-wound in his face, a janissary gave the Prince of Savoy a sword cut that clove his helmet. Eugene, turning quickly, plunged his sword deep into the Turk's breast. At that instant a musket-ball penetrated his leg just above the knee, and he dropped, still urging the attacking troops on to victory. He was removed from the field, and soon the joyful news was brought to him that Belgrade was taken.

The Prince's wound was extremely dangerous, for the ball could not be found for some time; and several months afterwards splinters of bone were removed from the leg. Everything was done that science could accomplish; Duke Victor Amadeus the Second sent his own physician to Vienna. Later a lung trouble developed; and it was not until January of the year 1689 that the Prince could journey to Turin to thank his cousin personally for all the kindness and sympathy which had been shown him.

The victories of the Austrian Emperor over the Turks had aroused tremendous jealousy at the court of Versailles. Louis, "the Most Christian King," instead of assisting in the defence, was much cast down at the defeat of the Turks, for he could not bear to see a powerful German Emperor as a rival. He now conceived a new plan and suddenly attacked the Emperor and his strongholds. As both were unprepared, he was very successful. Philippsburg fell; Mayence opened its gates to him; and with the connivance of the traitor Fürstenberg, coadjutor of the Cologne bishopric, Bonn, Kaiserswerth, and other fortified places passed into the hands of the French. After these great victories over the Turks, Emperor Leopold should have made peace with them and turned all his energies against the French, an opinion shared by all the princes of the empire. Incredible as it may seem, he did not do this, and as a consequence suddenly found himself between two enemies. Now he had all he could do to save his skin. It was a desperate situation; the hearts of German patriots, and there were plenty at this unfortunate time, were very heavy.

While Louis let loose in the Rhine provinces his marauding bands, which plundered and burned more than a hundred villages (the empty window-frames of Heidelberg Castle still testify to the shameful deeds of the French), he allied himself also with the Duke of Savoy. He believed it possible to make that country a point of vantage for attacks on the Germans, although it was a somewhat roundabout route. This was a very unpleasant surprise to the Duke of Savoy. He would much have preferred to keep quiet, a neutral observer of the bloody game of war. But there was no choice. He was obliged to decide and place himself either on the

Austrian side or else to make common cause with the French. With a heavy heart, as is natural with weak characters, he decided for the former. Eugene had labored hard with him—had represented to him all that the family of Carignan had suffered from the French, and what would befall him should he become a vassal of King Louis.

That decided him. A small German army (5,000 men) under the leadership of Caprara, Eugene with them, entered Savoy; and as Spanish troops soon came to their assistance, they confidently hoped to discipline the arrogant French. But it turned out differently. The Duke of Savoy played false, was bought by French money, and betrayed all the plans of the imperial leaders to the French general Catinat. He permitted the dangerous bandit warfare of the Piedmontese, the notorious sharp-shooters of modern times, against the Austrians. The soldiers were given poisoned food, several were murdered, small groups of them were attacked, and even the life of Eugene, who meanwhile had become a general of cavalry, was conspired against. A troop of at least one thousand men attempted to overwhelm his camp, but were bravely routed by the Taaffe regiment.

It was difficult for Eugene to believe in the perfidy of his uncle, whom he had truly loved and honored. But the proofs accumulated. At last he had an understanding with him, reproached him with his treachery, and begged him urgently to desist and to remain firmly attached to the Emperor's cause. The Duke, who wished to aggrandize his domain, and saw more advantage to himself through alliance with France rather than with Austria, did not listen to this advice but remained, as before, the secret ally of the King of France; thus he did more harm to the Austrian cause than a strongly armed enemy would have done.

The war continued with varying success until the year 1696. But it brought one real satisfaction to Eugene; he kept his promise to himself and from the Savoy mountains he entered France sword in hand, at the head of an army. He had occupied many French towns, when he received orders to retire to Milanese territory. He obeyed with a light heart, for an open-hearted, honest man is always at a disadvantage against cunning, malignity, treachery, and assassination. In Vienna an exceedingly gracious and brilliant reception awaited him. No one thought of blaming him for the ill success in Savoy. He had done all that it was possible to do. He became more and more devoted to the Emperor and to the German cause; he wished to give loyalty for loyalty.

Chapter IV
The Battle of Zenta

In the year 1697 we find Prince Eugene a Field-Marshal. How did he arrive so quickly at such high honors?

Old Count von Starhemberg, at that time president of the Imperial Council of War, had recommended him to the Emperor with the words: "I know of no one who possesses more understanding, experience, industry, and zeal in the Emperor's service, no one who is more generous and unselfish, or who possesses the love of the soldiery to a higher degree, than Prince Eugene of Savoy." This was a recommendation which carried great weight, above all from the mouth of so brave, thorough, and experienced a soldier as old Starhemberg, the valiant defender of Vienna. It was a time also when such a well recommended man could be very useful.

All was quiet in Italy, to be sure; the campaign on the Rhine was not being very actively conducted; but in Hungary the arch-enemy of Christendom threatened anew, and Eugene was the real scourge of the Turks. This warlike nation had, in more recent years, gained the ascendency through the breaking up of the imperial forces. The Elector of Saxony, Frederick August the Second, as the Emperor's commander-in-chief, had not been man enough to hold them back or destroy them. Fortunately, just at the right time, he was relieved of the command of the army, by accepting the throne of Poland. In this position he injured the German cause far less than he might have done as a soldier. When the Emperor's troops in Hungary learned that Prince Eugene was to command them again, there was loud rejoicing. Starhemberg's words about the love of the soldiers for him had already proved themselves true. It was really from this time that Eugene began his victorious career. He had now to depend solely on himself; upon his own powers, his own genius, and had no one above or beside him to tie his hands.

It must not be forgotten that Belgrade had again been taken from the Emperor. The Viennese Council of War did not consider it prudent, just then, to attempt its recapture, although Eugene would certainly have accomplished the task. It was far more necessary to furnish the half-starved army with provisions and clothing, and to improve the very loose discipline. For this latter task Eugene, with all his mildness, was well fitted—for the soldiers loved the thirty-two-year-old Field-Marshal like a father, and love makes obedience easy. Eugene gathered the scattered army together into camp at Cobila. Here he learned that the Turkish ruler, Mustapha the

Second, was in Belgrade and had built bridges over the rivers Danube and Save.

It was the universal opinion in the army that the Turks intended to cross the Save and attack Peterwardein. Eugene was the only one who understood the situation. He saw that the Turks had quite a different plan, and intended to push forward by forced marches toward Siebenbürgen to attack the eight Austrian regiments under General Rabutin, who were coming up. Leaving a sufficiently strong corps behind to observe the enemy, Eugene marched with the greater part of his forces along the Theiss to meet Rabutin.

It turned out splendidly; the meeting took place; and now Eugene determined to return to Peterwardein to defend this fortress against possible attacks of the enemy. He arrived there just in time to prevent the Turks from destroying the bridges over the marshes at St. Thomas-Syreck. A cheerful and courageous spirit prevailed throughout the army; the confidence of the leader communicated itself to each individual soldier. Eugene had good spies and scouts, those necessary evils of the army even down to our day. From one of them he learned that the Turks were going to advance on Szegedin, take the city and then hurry on to Siebenbürgen.

As this had to be prevented under all circumstances, Eugene hurried forward so quickly by forced marches, that by the twelfth of September he was within a mile of the enemy. He determined to attack at once. You should have seen the former little *abbé* or Capuchin now! The thought of fighting his first battle independently, without interference from any one, developed in the highest degree all the latent resources of his genius. He was equally ready in decision and in execution, and still his plans were so well considered and to the point that, as an eye witness declared, "there was no loophole for the goddess of chance to decide the day against him."

Scarcely had Eugene completed the placing of his army when a part of the Turkish cavalry made a descent upon him. To repulse them with great loss was an easy matter. And now the cannon began to roar from all sides—a terrible concert. One could see, from the continuous cloud of dust in the Turkish camp, that the Austrians were hitting the mark. After a sharp bombardment, the command was given, "Forward! march!" The Turkish intrenchments had to be taken in spite of a heavy fire from the enemy's lines. It was a bloody piece of work in which many a brave soldier bit the dust. Very likely the columns sometimes hesitated, but a glance at their brave leaders, their beloved Prince Eugene at the head, urged them forward. During this advance toward the enemy's front, Eugene had ordered the left wing of the army, under Starhemberg, to open a passage into the enemy's camp across the sandbars of the Theiss.

In spite of the desperate defence of the janissaries who, attacked from the rear, fought with the courage of despair, they were forced back step by step. The Austrian lines reached the intrenchments, which they carried with a rush and then began to scale the walls. To heighten the courage of his soldiers still more, Eugene himself led the cavalry regiment Styrum into the fight. Once more a terrific conflict broke out at the barricades, once more success seemed doubtful. There was less and less room for the cavalry to operate; there was nothing left but to leave the outcome to the already decimated infantry. But this the cavalry did not wish to do; they wanted to claim a share in the honors of victory. Like lightning they dismounted, mingling with the rapidly advancing infantry, and together they threw themselves against the intrenchments.

The janissaries saw that they were lost, but they resolved to sell their lives dearly. They threw away their muskets and drew their sabres. A short but terrible carnage began, man to man, eye to eye. The Emperor's troops in the majority, holding the advantage on every side, did terrible destruction. At last, with cries like wild animals, the janissaries turned for flight; all was not lost—the outlet over the bridge was still open. Horrible delusion! The general's eye had not failed here. The road to the bridge had long since been cut off—no outlet in any direction, no help! In wild confusion the Turks swarmed the rocky banks of the Theiss, where they were pushed, crowded by their own numbers and driven into the water by the Austrians with loud cries of victory, and thus most of them perished in the river. Terrible conflicts such as these took place all over the battle-field. Drunk with victory, the soldiers seemed to crave blood. With cries of: "This for Vienna!" "This for Buda!" "This for Belgrade!" they gave no quarter, and scorned the highest ransoms offered in order to take vengeance on their ancient enemies.

It was only nightfall which ended this bloody battle. Twenty thousand Turks lay dead or wounded on the field, ten thousand had found death in the wild waters of the Theiss. Barely a thousand had fled to the opposite shore, whence the Sultan watched the destruction of the faithful; the tragic end of his hopes. In the fear that his retreat toward Temesvar might be cut off by the Austrian troops, he rode away in the night on a fleet steed, accompanied by only a small band.

Messengers of victory hurried to Vienna. In his report to the Emperor, Eugene picturesquely said: "Even the sun would not set, until it had seen the complete triumph of the imperial arms." And the great general added: "Next to God's help, the victory at Zenta is to be ascribed to the heroic spirit of the leaders and soldiers." This modest soldier said not a word about himself and yet he had been the soul of it all. His military keenness, the boldness of his decisions, and not least of all, the energy with which he had carried out his plans on this day—which will always be a glorious one in Austrian annals—redound to his highest fame.

Eugene's fame spread on the wings of the wind over the whole of Germany and of Europe. He was classed with the greatest generals and even his enemies said, "This has been a miracle."

What must King Louis the Fourteenth and Louvois have thought of this? Perhaps they may have had a presentiment that some day France herself might be in his power.

The following day Eugene led the victorious army into the deserted camp of the Sultan. Here they discovered treasures beyond belief. Besides three million piastres in the war chest, they found an immense quantity of all kinds of weapons, all the ammunition and baggage, whole herds of camels, oxen, and sheep, and a great number of flags, horsetails, standards, and other trophies of war.

Such a victory as this at Zenta had never been won by Christians over unbelievers, and the heathen had never before suffered such a terrible defeat. It was now necessary to follow up the victory and to gather the fruits of it. The way in which Eugene contrived to do this in spite of many drawbacks and hindrances serves but to add another glorious leaf to his victor's wreath. In short, in a single campaign he had reconquered Siebenbürgen, Hungary as far as Temesvar, also Banat and Slavonia as far as Belgrade for his Emperor.

At the end of November Eugene returned to Vienna. The Emperor received him with every mark of favor and gratitude, and presented him with a sword richly set with precious stones. The populace enthusiastically greeted the famous conqueror of the Turks. He who had already so often repulsed the infidels had now exceeded their wildest hopes. Eugene became the people's hero and ever remained so.

On the twenty-sixth of January, 1699, peace was declared between the Emperor and the Porte, after seventy-two days of negotiations at Carlovitz, a little town near Peterwardein. This consummation, ardently desired by conquerors and conquered, had been brought about by Eugene.

The time of peace was taken advantage of by the Prince to found a home for himself in Vienna. This had long been his secret wish so that he could live quietly and devote himself to scientific study, for which he was more and more inclined. The house which he bought stood in the street called "Gate of Heaven," in the same place where later he built his new palace Belvedere, at present the seat of the Ministry of Finance. The Emperor also presented him with important estates in Hungary, and the Prince bought others for a mere song. There were now great hopes for an extended period of peace. The sound of arms had died away in the West as well as in the East, and even the mischief-maker, King Louis the Fourteenth, was eager to bequeath to his people the memory of a peace-loving ruler. The world drew a long breath, but alas—all too soon, to be again plunged into fresh disorders and new alarms of war.

Chapter V
War of the Spanish Succession

King Charles the Second of Spain died on the first of November, 1700, without leaving a natural heir to the throne. He was the last Hapsburg of the older line, and so they flattered themselves at the castle in Vienna that they could take this rich inheritance as a natural right. A sad disappointment awaited them. Charles the Second had, at the last moment, made a will in favor of France, appointing the grandson of the King, Duke Philip of Anjou, sole heir. It was very evident how this had been accomplished. Louis the Fourteenth had schemed and intrigued to get this rich inheritance for his family, and King Charles the Second of Spain was a weak character.

When the news reached Vienna it caused the greatest consternation, not only at court, but among all classes of the population. The people rioted in the streets of the capital; the ministers demanded that the Emperor should suppress the disorder; and the Crown Prince, Joseph the First, an active and passionate young man, went so far as to send for the French minister, the Marquis de Villars, and to denounce this proceeding of his master as underhanded and deceitful.

It was not to be wondered at that war soon broke out; the bloody War of the Spanish Succession, which lasted from 1700 to 1714, humbled, indeed, the arrogant Louis, and also inflicted great harm upon Germany. It is remarkable that one hundred and seventy years later the throne of Spain was again the bone of contention, and that it was again a French sovereign who was most concerned in the affair. This later ruler was chastised much more promptly and more thoroughly than his ancestor.

Crafty Louis the Fourteenth understood how to gain allies rapidly. These were the hypocritical Elector of Cologne, the Duke of Savoy, and unfortunately also the German Emperor's own son-in-law, the warlike and fiery Elector, Max Emanuel of Bavaria, the conqueror of Belgrade. They were all seduced by the vain promises of the French King that a crumb from the French inheritance should fall to them, and they lent a hand to the false ruler on the Seine, to war against the imperial house. The Emperor, on the other hand, stood quite alone, an almost pathetic figure in the great drama about to be enacted, but resolved from the bottom of his heart to risk everything in support of his rights.

The French were more enterprising than the Germans. While the recruiting drum was still heard in the crown-lands of Austria and warlike bands were still streaming in from all sides, not forgetting the imperial troops grown gray in the service and fresh from the Turkish wars, the French had already entered Italy in order to occupy the Spanish possessions in the spirit of the old adage, "Possession is nine points of the law." Starhemberg mobilized the imperial army in the Tyrol. It was a matter of course that the Field-Marshal Prince Eugene of Savoy should command it. Associated with him were two experienced French soldiers, two brothers-in-arms, the Prince de Commercy and the Prince de Vaudemont.

With thirty thousand men, "amongst them not one coward," as Eugene assured the Austrian Crown-Prince Joseph, Starhemberg and Börner advanced into Italy. On the twentieth of May, 1701, Eugene joined them at Roveredo. The French were commanded by Marshal Catinat—Eugene had once before, as we know, met him face to face in Italy. Catinat had made good use of his time and occupied all the mountain passes which led out of the Tyrol into Italy. The republic of Venice then held the eastern half of upper Italy. Under these circumstances many of the bravest and best heads in the army were very dubious about attacking the French. But Eugene was willing to take the responsibility; for such emergencies, he thought, the Emperor had made him a field-marshal. He was in very good spirits. Now the time had come to strike a blow at the French and especially at King Louis.

How different was his present position in Italy compared with that which he had occupied during his first campaign! He was now completely independent. The vain and crafty Catinat must be shown what he had learned, and he must uphold the glory of the German arms for the discomfiture of Louis. He must enter Italy, that was certain; and he knew how thoroughly Catinat had intrenched himself. Eugene quickly made up his mind; he absolutely must attack him; he had not studied the tactics of the great Carthaginian, Hannibal, for nothing. Like him, he chose a passage over the Alps. For this enterprise alone, had he fought no other battles, nor rendered any other service to the Emperor and the country, Eugene would have gained immortal renown. All the more so, as at that time many of the facilities were entirely lacking which would now be at the service of a general.

And how did he accomplish this daring feat? Thousands of soldiers and inhabitants of the surrounding country were kept busy early and late making a passageway for the troops over the steep mountain paths. Here a shoulder of rock was broken away with shovels, pickaxes, and crowbars; there a steep declivity was graded; at another place a dam was made out of great logs, or a bridge was built over a gorge. Withal Eugene's greatest task was to keep Catinat in ignorance of the road which he was preparing, although the Frenchman could scarcely dream of the possibility of such a surprise.

He kept General von Guttenstein constantly before the French army so that Catinat should think that Eugene's position was just behind the General's vanguard.

Early on the morning of May 26 the march began, which was to equal the most celebrated feats of this kind in ancient as well as modern times, and indeed to surpass most of them. The army advanced in two sections and by two different roads. The dragoons who were delegated to accompany the infantry had to dismount and lead their horses by the bridles. The cannon were hoisted with ropes, and the wagons were taken apart and carried. Arrived at the top, the cannon were drawn by oxen, while soldiers and peasants walked beside them to keep them from sliding off the paths or to lend a hand where the road was steep. In places where a cart had never crossed these inaccessible mountains, a whole army now found passage. In the best of spirits the soldiers moved forward, delighted with this silent and beautiful world, past dizzy precipices and yawning depths, through virgin forests and rough moraines.

By the fourth of June, Eugene with the whole Austrian army had achieved the "surmounted impossibility" as he jokingly called this daring alpine march, and Catinat was greatly astonished to see him appear before him with his 30,000 men. He was already half beaten, for with the enemy so close at hand, he could not make up his mind which plan to choose. He spread his troops along the river Etsch, fatigued them with constant marching and countermarching, expected an attack first in this quarter, then in that, and did not know what to do—quite a contrast to Eugene, who had long ago made up his mind what course to take.

At last the decisive moment came. In the night, between the eighth and ninth of July, Eugene crossed the Tartaro with 11,000 men and made a sharp attack upon the enemy intrenched at Castagnaro. The Austrians fought like lions. It was not long before the place was taken and the French expelled. From there, Eugene marched his whole force against the town of Carpi. He met indeed with great difficulties in this territory, which was intersected by canals, morasses, ricefields, and brush, but he managed to overcome them all. The armies were soon to measure their strength once more. One side fought as bravely as the other. Eugene's horse was shot under him, and he received a slight wound, in spite of which he led his troops on to victory at Carpi. Inspired by his previous successes, he developed an enterprise, a daring of conception, and a facility in carrying out his plans, which made this one of his most brilliant campaigns.

On the twenty-seventh of July he crossed the Mincio, to Catinat's great alarm. After this movement Catinat had but one thought, to reach the Oglio, where, covered by this river, he might prevent the Austrians from entering Milanese territory. On this retreat the French proved themselves true barbarians. They laid waste the country wherever they could, burned and plundered shamelessly, but in revenge many of these robbers were shot down by the embittered peasantry. The Austrian soldiers who followed them were greeted as deliverers from the French yoke.

In Paris there was great consternation over the misfortunes of Marshal Catinat. Proud King Louis had counted on victory and here was nothing but Job's comfort. But what provoked him most was the fact that it was the little *abbé* with the disagreeable face who had gained these victories over his troops. To mend the situation and ensure success for the future, after recalling Catinat, the King's former playmate and intimate friend, Marshal Villeroi, was intrusted with the command of the army in Italy. He boasted that he would soon drive Eugene back into the Tyrolese mountains, and promised the Parisians that he would teach three Princes (Eugene, Commercy, and Vaudemont) to dance to his piping, and even that he would send them back prisoners to the French capital.

In the beginning he really seemed formidable, for he brought fresh troops to Italy, so that he outnumbered the Austrians, two to one. His first move was to reoccupy the left bank of the Oglio. Prince Eugene had good reasons for not interfering, which Villeroi with truly comic shortsightedness characterized as "a sign of weakness and fear." But Eugene understood very well what he was doing and what remained to be done. He now took up an excellent position with his troops facing in three directions, placed his cannon in a masterly manner, and thought to himself: "If you want anything of me, I am ready for you!"

And they came. It was on the first of September, 1701, at the little town of Chiari. With the greatest ease the Austrian outposts were carried and, with the fiery impetuosity which is peculiar to the French in a first assault, they advanced against Eugene's intrenchments. To their great surprise they saw scarcely a man, for Eugene had ordered his soldiers to lie down behind their redoubts and not to fire until the enemy were within fifty feet. Many a brave soldier's fingers, as he watched the advance of the French, may have itched to pull the trigger while they were still at a distance. But their beloved General had given the order and they never moved an eyelash! Suddenly the fire burst forth from all sides, and whole columns of the French were mowed down. Again the second and third ranks fired and the cannon fell in line with volleys of grapeshot. That was indeed a surprise. It was an awful massacre.

Marshal Villeroi was so disconcerted by this beginning that he did not know what to do next. He issued no orders and left his army unprotected under the adversaries' constant fire. It was his corps-commanders, Catinat and

Duke Victor Amadeus of Savoy, who arranged for the retreat of the army. Eugene did not remain passive, but drove the enemy out of every position, replacing them with his own men. At Chiari sixty thousand Frenchmen were vanquished by twenty-five thousand Germans. The enemy suffered a loss of over two thousand men, among them two hundred officers, while the Austrian army counted only thirty-six dead and eighty-one wounded. This was a cheap victory.

But besides their armed enemy the French had another enemy in the peasants of Lombardy. The country favored the Germans more each day. Every night wagon-loads of provisions were voluntarily sent to them, while the French began to suffer hunger and want. Added to this came continuous showers of rain, making impassable roads. In a few words Villeroi described the condition of the army to the King: "To remain here longer would be to ruin our fine cavalry." Thus quickly had the boastful Marshal changed his opinions and forgotten utterly his promise to teach the three princes to dance.

On the thirteenth of November the French retired once more across the Oglio. Eugene's batteries assisted them in a most unwelcome manner. He then sent out patrolling parties, who continually harassed them, giving them no time to take breath. He took Caneto from them and drove them out of the whole Mantuan territory. The city itself was still occupied by the French, but they could take no comfort in it, for Prince Eugene had it well blockaded and watched night and day. Eugene showed such tireless energy that it seemed as though he were just beginning the campaign instead of having already brought it to a glorious conclusion, thereby augmenting the power of the imperial house and gaining the affection and sympathy of the people. Now, one sovereign after another began to reflect that it might be better for his own interests if the Emperor, instead of Louis the Fourteenth of France, held the balance of power.

The first to decide in favor of the Emperor was the new King of Prussia, Frederick the First. He promised the Emperor to furnish an army of ten thousand men. Then came Denmark contributing six thousand men. Hanover also did not hold back. Still more important was it that England and Holland declared for the Emperor, of course in their own interests; for while France had the ascendancy they feared for their commerce with Spain and the East and West Indies.

Meanwhile Duke Victor Amadeus earned scant thanks in Turin for the help he had given. Though he had fought bravely at Chiari and had led his soldiers into the thick of the fight, yet he was under suspicion in Paris. All the misfortunes in Italy were attributed to him, and they would have been glad to put all the burden of failure on his shoulders. This the faithless

Savoy saw full well, but did not consider it the proper time to draw his threatened head out of the French noose, and he did not have the courage to declare openly for the Emperor.

Marshal Villeroi spent the winter in Cremona living care-free a life of pleasure and luxury. The three princes had long since heard of his promise to make them dance in Paris. They may have thought that it would be a good idea to make him dance in Vienna. These were amusing thoughts to while away the dreary hours of camp life, but were at first vague and without definite purpose. They would have liked best to take the whole nest, Cremona, with its rare bird. But just now there was no time; and besides this, all the means for a complete siege were lacking, although the desire for it grew greater from day to day.

One of the three, Prince Commercy, was a cunning fellow; when he had made up his mind to a thing it was not easy to dissuade him. He was the one who had been most annoyed by Villeroi's promise to the Parisians. He now concocted a plot, splendid in its way, which I shall describe to you. Field-Marshal Prince Commercy was already acquainted in Cremona from earlier times. A priest who lived there had been a companion of his student days at the University. They exchanged confidential letters, and one word led to another. Through this priest (Antonio Cosoli was his name) he learned casually that an old empty canal, which had been unnoticed by the French forces, intersected the fortifications and was connected with the cellar of the house owned by Father Cosoli. This fell in nicely with Commercy's plan. He immediately communicated the discovery to Prince Eugene, who took this opportunity of introducing his soldiers into the town, so that he might perhaps gain possession of it. He knew that the gates were not well guarded, and that there were even no sentries on the walls; all of which favored his undertaking.

On a pitch dark January night, whose terrors were augmented by a storm of wind and rain, the troops which Eugene had selected for this surprise broke camp. There were grenadiers, cuirassiers, and hussars, altogether about four thousand men. Another somewhat smaller band was guided along the Po by Prince Vaudemont, to take the bridge by storm and enter the town by way of the river. Eugene, Commercy, and Starhemberg rode on ahead of their troops to a house about two thousand yards from Cremona. The troops should have arrived there at two o'clock in the morning, but were delayed until about five o'clock by the heavy rains and muddy roads. Major Hofman of the Geschwind regiment, led by a trusty guide, stole with his grenadiers through the long canal scarcely two feet broad, which had until this time served only as a refuge for the rats. He had orders to remain concealed in the priest's house until Colonel Count Nasary of the Lorraine regiment and Lieutenant-Colonel Count Knefstein of the Hebenstein regiment could likewise penetrate into the town by the same means. Hofman was to overcome the guard at the Margaret Gate as quietly as possible, to open the gate, and then by means of three columns of fire on the walls, to give the signal for the advance of the troops outside. Lieutenant-Colonel Count Mercy was commanded then to enter the city, gallop to the Po Gate, and open it for Vaudemont.

The plan succeeded perfectly. The French guard was overcome and the gate opened. In full gallop with drawn sabres the German cavalry dashed through the streets to the appointed places. The infantry took the important posts, and Eugene with his staff betook himself to the court-house, to direct the further movements of the troops from there. There was but one more thing to do: it was necessary to hold themselves on the defensive until Prince Vaudemont had surprised the bridge, to throw open the gates for him, and then with united forces to compel the enemy to surrender or to annihilate them.

Marshal Villeroi had returned in the evening from Milan, where he had doubtless eaten and drunk well, and he was now sleeping like a dormouse. It was not until seven o'clock in the morning that a few musket shots were heard near his quarters. Drunk with sleep, the Frenchman turned over in bed. A lackey broke into his room with the terrible cry, "The Germans are in the city!"

You should have seen the Marshal jump up then! He was in great haste! He quickly threw on some clothes and sprang upon his horse. Too late! At that moment German soldiers saw him and pulled him down. They squabbled over him, for they suspected a lucky catch and each wanted to claim him. Just then an officer, the Irishman MacDonald, threw himself upon the struggling soldiers and freed Villeroi from his painful predicament. The Marshal offered him ten thousand pistoles and a regiment in the French army, if he would allow him to escape. Now for the first time the Irishman perceived what a rare bird he had in his snare, but the loyal fellow refused these brilliant offers and led his captive to headquarters.

Starhemberg recognized Villeroi immediately, received his sword, and then sent him to Prince Eugene. In spite of the seriousness of the situation it must have been a merry meeting. The spectacular drama "three dancing princes" had come to naught, and the Parisians would have to forego this promised pleasure. Instead Marshal Villeroi was marched away to Ustiano.

In the meantime the shooting, drumming, and shouting in Cremona had grown so loud that the French realized what had happened. One of their officers, who was just about to lead his battalion to the parade ground, threw himself heroically on the Germans and so gave his countrymen time to assemble. In spite of this, they would have been conquered if Prince

Vaudemont had arrived from the Po Gate, which Count Mercy had opened for him. But here a very desperate fight had taken place. Two Irish regiments in the French service had attacked brave Mercy, taken him prisoner, and burned the bridge over the Po, thus preventing Vaudemont from crossing the river.

The French had now retired into the houses and from thence kept up a well-directed fire on the Austrians. Hour after hour the battle wavered; the Austrians began to run short of ammunition. Besides this, Eugene was afraid of being cut off from his line of retreat by General Crequi, who was probably marching toward Cremona. Therefore at five o'clock in the afternoon, as twilight began to fall, he gave orders to evacuate the city. He took with him as prisoners nineteen officers, four hundred soldiers, seven standards, and five hundred horses. Besides this, the French lost twelve hundred dead and wounded in the streets of the city, while the Emperor's troops lost only six hundred. Marshal de Villeroi was taken to Graz, where he was held for nine months and well treated, then exchanged without any ransom for a Count Waldstein, who had been taken by the French at Carpi. The French proclaimed Eugene's retreat from Cremona as a victory for themselves and composed couplets in which they congratulated themselves on having held Cremona and having lost Villeroi.

The French King now appointed Duke Louis of Vendôme in Villeroi's place. Louis and Eugene had formerly been playmates. Both had had an honorable career and were now to play at the terrible game of war as opponents. They appreciated one another's talents also; at least Eugene frankly said that Vendôme was a formidable antagonist.

But the game was now quite a different one. Vendôme's army, through new accessions, numbered nearly eighty thousand; Eugene had, as before, his thirty thousand. How was it possible to achieve success, as Vendôme was constantly on the alert and was determined to make good the mistakes of his predecessors, Catinat and Villeroi? Besides this, Eugene's army began to need money, arms, and clothing. The Council-of-War in Vienna replied to his urgent demands only with embarrassed shrugs. The old president of the council, Ehren-Starhemberg, had passed away, and the other gentlemen were perhaps not so well disposed toward the young Field-Marshal, who had been promoted so rapidly. Therefore it was all the more necessary that Eugene should keep cool and take every possible precaution. But one must have the means to execute as well as the brain to plan, in order to be successful. And the means were now sadly lacking, so that Eugene was obliged to keep very quiet and avoid an engagement for the present, that the enemy might not have an opportunity of destroying him; for the Frenchman was very anxious to distinguish himself by a brilliant coup. And now Eugene conceived a clever plan. Should it succeed, it would be something to capture Vendôme, even if he could not cripple his army. Through a loyal Piedmontese, Eugene had learned that Vendôme occupied a house which stood quite alone on the Lake of Mantua. It should be an easy task to approach by water, to surprise the Marshal and carry him off in a boat to the opposite shore into Eugene's camp. He lost no time in carrying out this enterprise. On a mild June night twelve boats carrying two hundred picked men under Marquis Daria were launched. They moved cautiously and silently forward. On arriving, Daria disembarked with a few soldiers and called out to the sentry that he had brought some sick Frenchmen from Mantua. Instead of beating down the sentry, as had been commanded, one of the soldiers with unpardonable zeal fired upon him, and the comrades who had remained behind in the boats also began firing. This made such a terrific uproar that Daria thought it best to retire as quickly as possible.

Thus unfortunately, this attempt, which with a little more caution might have turned out so well, failed. Eugene was highly indignant, caused a rigid investigation to be made, and the guilty ones were well punished. Vendôme was so angry at the attempt to take him prisoner and send him to Vienna that he shelled the Austrian camp, but could not prevent Eugene from taking his revenge by surrounding Mantua with redoubts.

Soon after these events Eugene's army suffered a hard blow, due likewise to the great carelessness of the higher officers. Austrian cavalry had driven back the enemy to the Crostolo. At Santa Vittoria they took up a position which, on reconnoitring, Eugene found to be very insecure. He turned over the command of the cavalry to the master of ammunition, Count Auersperg, although he seemed to have a premonition of disaster. Auersperg conducted the affair with the most unpardonable carelessness, placed no sentries, and neglected every precaution. Of course disaster followed. Vendôme took him by surprise, and so sudden and unexpected was the attack that the men did not even have time to seize their horses and mount. Now, too late, Auersperg sought to repair his mistakes. He rallied his soldiers about him and, scorning death, placed himself at their head and managed to drive the enemy back, and even to take some standards from them. The French infantry, however, advanced and commenced a murderous musketry fire, which the cavalry was not long able to endure. They turned for flight. Many tried to swim the Tassone, but were carried away by the current or found death on its marshy banks. A wild charge of the dragoon regiment, Herbeville, then drove back the enemy and rescued the scattered and fleeing comrades.

At eleven o'clock in the evening, Eugene learned of the unfortunate occurrence. He immediately took all precautions to prevent the enemy from making any further advance. Indeed he soon did still more: he retrieved this disaster by the battle at Luzzara on the Po, on the first of August, 1702. At that place Vendôme occupied an excellent position protected by dams, moats, and barricades. The battle did not begin until nearly five o'clock in the afternoon. Twenty-four thousand Germans were opposed to fifty-three thousand Frenchmen.

Eugene's army was divided into two columns, one of them led by Starhemberg, the other by Field-Marshal Prince de Commercy. The latter opened the battle. His soldiers threw themselves upon the enemy from a dam, behind which they had been concealed, and were received with a terrible hail of shot. On horseback, within sight of all his men, Commercy remained in the thick of the fight. Suddenly—hit by two balls at once—the hero fell from his horse, dead. His men hesitated and gave way. This made a dangerous breach. But Eugene's keen eye guided the battle. Two imperial regiments and the Danes hurried up to their support. Backward and forward surged the battle. Success seemed out of the question. Then Eugene himself came dashing up. With that bold disregard of death which was characteristic of the hero, he put himself at the head of his men and led them forward once more. In a solid column the battalions advanced. Nothing could restrain their heroic ardor. They climbed the dike and threw the enemy back on their camp.

On the left wing of the imperial army, commanded by Starhemberg, the fighting was even more bitter. Opposed to him was the flower of the French troops under Vendôme's own leadership. With impetuous courage Starhemberg pushed forward. Nothing could withstand him. He drove the enemy before him in a rout. It seemed as though they were becoming demoralized; the French retreat looked like flight. In the zeal of the pursuit a wide gap was made in the ranks of the Austrians. As Eugene had done, Vendôme now recognized the great danger to his right wing. He formed, from the reserves and several other regiments, a tremendous storming column, which he hurriedly threw upon the Starhemberg troops, who were already drunk with victory. He broke through their front ranks and forced the whole wing into a hurried retreat. Disaster was imminent and only timely and effective assistance could save the day. At the decisive moment Prince Vaudemont came rattling up with his heavy cavalry. This successful attack gave Starhemberg time to re-form his regiments and to push on to a renewed assault. This took place with great effect, supported by the well-aimed fire of Börner's artillery. Although the French did their best to hold their ground—53,000 against 24,000—it was of no use, they were obliged to retire into their protected camp. Eugene's plan was to storm this immediately and drive out the French. But his regiments were so exhausted that the setting sun counselled both struggling parties to take a much needed rest.

The day at Luzzara placed a new leaf in Eugene's victor's wreath, although Vendôme and later prejudiced historians would like so well to dispute this. The French celebrated the day as a victory, fired salutes and caused the bells to be rung in Cremona and Milan. In his quiet fashion Eugene comments upon this: "One should allow them to shout a little, as the innkeeper does his guests when they have settled their accounts." This comment of the General passed from mouth to mouth and described the situation perfectly. The fact was, however, that it was the Austrians who held possession of the battle-field, and even on the next day and the following ones Vendôme contented himself with sending a cannon ball now and then among the Austrians. If he was not badly beaten at Luzzara, why did he not again attack Eugene and his handful of men? Why did he not follow up his victory?

For the present no new enterprises were undertaken in Italy. The Frenchmen lacked courage and the Austrians the money for them. In Eugene's own words: the want of everything was much greater than he could describe or one could believe who had not himself seen it; and in the war office in Vienna there were words but no funds, which are the sinews of war.

Chapter VI
Blenheim

In the year 1703 Prince Eugene was appointed President of the Royal Council of War in Vienna, a position which placed him at the head of all military affairs. This was a very happy choice. Eugene was just the man to bring order into affairs and to act with decision. Things were at loose ends, as the reader may have noticed. In accepting this high honor from the Emperor, Eugene had made but one condition; namely, that he should be strongly supported in all his measures for the good of the service and the army. A field was now opened to him where his keenness and insight found their proper activities. The troops rejoiced greatly at the promotion of their beloved leader. They forgot the trials they had suffered, and hoped for better days. They believed that, now, at least they would not be obliged to suffer for necessities.

The Emperor was in dire need of a competent minister of war; of a brain which could plan for all. Within a short time the condition of European affairs had changed completely, and though the Emperor's cause was greatly helped by the recent acquisition of powerful allies, still there were so many complicated threads that it would take a very clever hand to untangle them, to organize the different divisions of the army, and to guide and hold them ready for prompt and decisive action. That this would not be an easy task was self-evident. Prince Eugene, like all mortals, had his enemies and detractors. His energetic methods did not please everyone, especially those in higher circles, who had heretofore been indifferent and passive. The situation must have caused him many a headache. But there was one thing that supported him; namely, devotion to his Emperor and his righteous cause, to promote which he tirelessly considered new plans and means which involved many little vexations and mortifications. "Patience! patience! patience!" he often said to himself. He generally proposed the opposite of that which he really intended, knowing beforehand that his suggestion would be rejected and that the measure which he himself really wanted would be recommended. It was a remarkable and dangerous game which his colleagues were playing while the glorious continuation or the shameful downfall of the German imperial house hung in the balance!

As we already know, England and Holland had taken sides with the hard-pressed German Emperor and had placed a strong army in the Netherlands. Their commander was the gifted English General Marlborough, who had already met the French several times and had shown them that he knew how to conduct a war and understood the arts of attack and defence equally well. With a second army Margrave Louis of Baden stood guard over the Rhine in the neighborhood of his home, and the Prussian allies were also on hand under the leadership of the daring Prince Leopold of Dessau. Unfortunately the Elector Max Emanuel of Bavaria was still on the French side. Guided by petty self-interest, he had deserted and betrayed his German fatherland.

Besides the French and Bavarians, the Turks and Hungarians were bestirring themselves once more. This was a prearranged scheme in which France again had her hand, for she was anxious to attack Austria from all sides. But the outcome was very different from what the Emperor's enemies had expected. We shall see what happened.

The two generals, Marlborough and Eugene, were placed first in command. For a long time they had been mutual admirers. They were attracted to one another, for, as the maxim says: like seeks like. Eugene, who was thoroughly German in feeling, was deeply pained to know that the French were in Germany—that is, in Bavaria. Had he had the power he would soon have turned them out. He now devised a plan by means of which, with the aid of the English, he might accomplish this. It may be admitted that there had been a great deal of correspondence in regard to the matter, but when it had been thoroughly considered in all its details it was remarkable how well the plans of the two generals coincided.

Eugene and Marlborough's plan in brief was, to unite their forces in Bavaria, to call also upon Margrave Louis of Baden, and then to strike a sudden blow. For the present Prince Eugene temporarily resigned his office of President of the Council of War, donned his modest soldier's coat, and girded on his sword. As the direct road was occupied by the Bavarians and French—the latter under Marshal Marsin—he hurried to the seat of war by the roundabout way of the Tyrol and Vorarlberg. His arrival was greeted with loud rejoicings by the army. Those princes who were allied in opposition to the imperial house felt that his appearance was the forerunner of important events. For instance, the Elector of Bavaria wrote to the King of France: "It is not to be doubted that the Prince of Savoy visits the seat of war in order to carry out great projects." It was plain that his opponents feared the noble knight. Had Margrave Louis of Baden been as resolute as of old, it would certainly have been an easy task for him to make the Elector of Bavaria, who was just now separated from Marsin, feel the sharpness of his sword. As it was, he pursued him but tardily and confronted him at last at Ehingen, near Ulm, where the Elector was encamped.

It was at this time that Eugene rejoined the army. He could probably not avoid reproaching the Margrave, though this must have been a very unpleasant task, for he was much indebted to him; but the service could not be allowed to suffer through friendship. However, all might yet be well. Marlborough was on the way to southern Germany with his army, consisting of picked troops, excellently clothed and armed. He had sent word to Eugene that he would conquer or die with him.

On the tenth of June, 1704, Eugene and Marlborough met for the first time at Mundelsheim. They made the most agreeable impression upon one another. A confidential intercourse developed and a mutual desire to accommodate one another in all points, which soon showed its happy effects on the soldiers of both armies.

Three days later they joined the Margrave of Baden at Grossheppach. To this day, at the inn "Zum Lamm" ("at the sign of the Lamb"), the tree is shown beneath which the three generals held a council of war. The resolution was taken to lure the enemy, now in southern Bavaria, across the Danube in order to destroy him.

The Margrave, as the higher in rank, insisted on taking command of the imperial troops and coöperating with Marlborough on the Danube. In order not to disturb the good understanding, Eugene subordinated himself and took command of the troops on the Rhine. This was a very important post, for it was necessary to prevent the union of the French marshals, Tallart and Villeroi, an attempt which Eugene from the first considered scarcely possible.

In increasing numbers the French pressed forward across the Rhine. They meant to give Germany her death-blow. Eugene's plan was to detain Villeroi on the Rhine, on his way from the Netherlands. In the meantime Marlborough and Louis of Baden had not been idle; the Bavarian Field-Marshal Arco, who with eight thousand men had attempted to dispute their passage of the Danube, had been crushed at the Schottenberg. As a result of this, the Elector retired to Augsburg. Under cover of its cannon he felt himself secure. The allies followed at his heels, but without attempting anything.

Efforts were again made toward peace, and an attempt was made to reconcile the Elector with his father-in-law, the Emperor.

All was in vain. The Elector, in his boundless ambition, planned first to tear the German Empire asunder and then to appropriate the lion's share. He again had visions of the crown of France, or indeed the German imperial crown, upon his head; he was, in short, a cheap creature of the "Most Christian" King of France, and would hear nothing of reconciliation. He did his utmost to hasten the advance of Marshal Tallart. War alone should decide his fate.

Tallart appeared, but close after him followed Eugene, whom Villeroi believed to be still at the Stollhof frontier. On the third of August the Prince was at Höchstädt, going into camp there and joining Marlborough a few days later. Margrave Louis of Baden had in the meantime undertaken the siege of Ingolstadt, so that his indecision could no longer be a hindrance.

Haste was now necessary; not a moment must be lost. Both great generals agreed that the decisive battle must be fought on the narrow plain between Blenheim and Höchstädt. To this end the enemy were allowed to cross the Danube quietly and establish themselves at Höchstädt. The Bavarians and French had no real knowledge of the true state of affairs. They intended to attack Eugene, whom they believed to be separated from Marlborough, and they expected to overcome him without much difficulty. Too late they learned their mistake.

From the church tower at Tapfheim Marlborough and Eugene observed the advance and manœuvres of the enemy. They posted themselves on the opposite side of the Nebelbach. The right wing rested on Blenheim on the Danube, where Tallart took up his quarters. The left wing, under Marsin, was supported by the village of Lutzingen and the slopes of the Goldberg. The Nebelbach was in front of them. The Elector with his cavalry was situated at Sonderheim, a short distance from Blenheim. The allies were behind the Kesselbach. Marlborough, who commanded the left wing, was at Münster on the Danube; Eugene, with the right, at Oppertshofen. Thus dawned the twelfth of August of the year 1704, the day which was to decide the power of German strength over French force and cunning.

As early as three o'clock in the morning the roll of drums and trumpet calls awakened the allies to the bloody harvest work of this hot August day. The moon was setting and threw its last pale light over the landscape. A thick fog covered the great plain and hid the distance. Each of the allies' armies was divided into four columns, of which two consisted of infantry and two of cavalry. The infantry marched in front, the cavalry behind, and the artillery was in the middle. A ninth column was formed to cover the march of the English and Dutch artillery, then to attack Blenheim and from thence to fall upon the enemy's right flank. The Prussian reserve corps, under the young Prince Leopold of Dessau, was attached to Eugene's army.

The fog lifted; it was nearly seven o'clock when the enemy became visible. They were still under the strange delusion that the allies would not dare to attack them, but would retire toward Nördlingen. But all at once they were surprised by a sudden onslaught. The Bavarian outposts were quickly overcome; the battle broke out here and there in jets of flame. In order to hold Blenheim, Tallart made the mistake of withdrawing twenty-seven battalions from his centre, where Clerambault commanded. The narrow strip between the village and the Danube was protected by a barricade of wagons, behind which stood four regiments of unmounted dragoons ready to defend it. The French line of battle was spread out for miles. It surged back and forth like the ebb and flow of the sea.

At nine o'clock in the morning Tallart's artillery opened a murderous fire on the allies, who, of course, answered in kind. Eugene's regiments, particularly, suffered under this fierce cannonading. Coming up from a hollow, their left flank was in line of the firing, but in spite of this they hastily threw five bridges across the Nebelbach.

Toward noon Marlborough mounted his horse and gave the signal for the attack. Lord Cutts proceeded with his men, at the signal for a general advance, toward the mills of Blenheim, and took them. At the same time the English cavalry crossed the Nebelbach. Immediately they were engaged in a hand to hand struggle with the French. There were mighty blows of the sword on helmet and armor; the squadrons plunged wildly upon one another. Unfortunately the English cavalry was the weaker. Pursued by the French they fell back on the infantry; but here the French advance was checked and whole ranks were mowed down by the English musketeers. New companies came storming up, only to meet the same fate, and all without any effect on the general result. The decisive struggle took place at Blenheim; but here at first every attack was in vain. Every garden wall, every hedgerow and fence, was prepared for defence; and the churchyard, which lay rather high, was transformed into a small citadel. Marlborough quickly changed his plan of attack. While he feigned attacks on Blenheim, his principal blow was struck at the enemy's centre, which Tallart had weakened considerably by sending reinforcements to Blenheim. But even here it was impossible to accomplish anything. The French fought with the courage of despair, and the English had to give way. At this decisive moment Marlborough placed himself at the head of the Danish troops, crossed the Nebelbach, and attacked the French again with fresh energy. Marsin's cavalry came dashing up and threw themselves heavily upon the Danes.

All was wild confusion; already the Danes were seeking a way for retreat, and all seemed lost. Just then the imperial cuirassiers, led by Fugger, came dashing up. With irresistible force they threw themselves upon the enemy, renewed the firing, and soon worsted the foe. The battle had been raging for hours and was still, on the whole, undecided. Eugene also had been fighting with the same ill success. With but eleven battalions of Prussians and seven battalions of Danes, he could scarcely make any headway. Once more, however, they put forth their utmost efforts. Such a bloody battle had never been known. The attack was begun by the Prussians under Leopold. It was a difficult piece of work. From Lutzingen the enemy's batteries poured death and destruction incessantly into their ranks. The brave grenadiers furiously threw themselves upon them and took them in a wild struggle. But the Bavarians were soon on the spot and the Prussians were driven back with great loss.

Eugene collected the scattered forces and placed himself at their head. The attack was unsuccessful. It was impossible for the eighteen battalions of infantry to wrest the victory from the twenty-five battalions of the Elector. Eugene now called on Marlborough for assistance, in expectation of which the Prince went into the ranks, encouraging the men, with word and example, to stand firm and have courage. But time pressed, and before Marlborough's reinforcements arrived the Prince had made a third attack. His keen soldier's eye had noted that the advantage was inclining toward Marlborough's side. Now all depended on cutting off the advance of the French right wing. The cavalry should have undertaken this, but were so disheartened by the repeated assaults that no great success was to be depended on. Full of disdain, Eugene turned his back on them and rode to the Prussian infantry. These did their duty completely. Regardless of danger they dashed forward under Eugene's leadership, while the Prince of Dessau encouraged his men to do the impossible. The grenadiers loaded and fired as carefully as though they were on the parade ground, and executed evolutions which made the hearts of old and young warriors laugh within them—until at last the enemy began to retire through the forest and by the ravine-road at Lutzingen. Here in the midst of this wild scrimmage Eugene nearly lost his life. A Bavarian cavalryman, who had probably recognized him, was taking aim with his carbine, when he was rendered harmless by an imperial officer who came hurrying up.

And still the battle raged. The Bavarians fought with the courage of lions and stood as firm as rocks amid the sea. At last news came from the other wing: Marlborough was gaining the advantage. Marshal Tallart had been wounded and taken prisoner, and Blenheim was surrounded by the English. Now the cowardly and treacherous Clerambault yielded his place, which was the key of the French position, and the English pushed into Blenheim, where they shot and cut down all who opposed them, and made nine thousand prisoners.

Marlborough's trumpet-calls of victory were the signal for Eugene also to make a quick end of things. With the last strength of his battalions and squadrons—Prince Leopold, with his Prussians, at the head—he at last compelled the enemy to retreat. But they gave way only by inches. The Bavarians still fought with the utmost tenacity, defending every foot of ground, until at last, completely weakened and shot to pieces, they succumbed to the fire of the Prussian infantry.

Thus the Germans had gained a great and important, but very bloody victory. Fifty-two thousand Germans and English had fought against fifty-six thousand French and Bavarians. Fourteen thousand of the latter now covered the battle-field, and nearly as many had been taken prisoners. The trophies consisted of one hundred and forty cannon and a great number of flags and standards. All Germany and the greater part of Europe rejoiced over the victory at Blenheim and the thorough humiliation and chastisement of the French. Marlborough and Eugene were the heroes of the day. The former was created a prince of the holy Roman empire by the Emperor, and Eugene's house in Vienna was made perpetually free of taxation as a privileged "freehouse" of the nobility.

In Paris, on the other hand, great discouragement reigned. Almost every important family mourned their dead or feared for a wounded or imprisoned son. The despondency was general. And again it was the former little *abbé* whose face was so distasteful to Louis the Fourteenth that had brought this misfortune upon him and his country. Had the allies pursued the French as fast as they fled toward the Rhine, the battle of Blenheim would have had still more important results. This was part of Eugene's plan; but in Vienna there was a group of extremely circumspect gentlemen who had very different views—"clerks and scribblers," as Blücher later named this distasteful guild.

Chapter VII
The Italian Campaign

The French now wished to make up in Italy what they had lost in Germany. The prospects for this seemed very good. The Hungarians, under the daring Count Alexander Karolyi, were gathering in the neighborhood of Vienna; while in Italy the imperial troops were starving.[4]

The Emperor Leopold the First had grown old and indifferent, and his characteristic indecision and lack of self-confidence had increased. The faithful artillery General, von Heister, drove the Hungarians before him, and Eugene was again sent to Italy to restore order and if possible clear the way. There was one favorable circumstance. His uncle, Duke Victor Amadeus, had at last broken his compact with the French and had come over to the Emperor's side. He had not received much benefit from his friendship with the French. "Hands off here, hands off there," had been the cry, and there was no regard for ties of relationship.

In Italy the two brothers, the Duke of Vendôme and the Grand Prior, were in command. Eugene had first to deal with the latter, who was not particularly brilliant. By means of marches and countermarches he kept him busy, eluding him cleverly when the Grand Prior thought to have surely entrapped him. But this could not long continue. Eugene soon became disgusted with the comedy. In August, 1705, he confronted the Grand Prior at the town of Cassano on the Adda. The position of the enemy was excellent, while Eugene, besides the eight thousand Prussians under Prince Leopold of Dessau, possessed but a small army. Still he wished to attack the Grand Prior, who had no idea that the enemy was so close until he was enlightened by messengers from his brother, the Duke. He was now all the more alert, fearing a severe reprimand. He placed his troops behind several canals and garrisoned the island in the Adda, as well as a large stone building which commanded the island and the bridge leading to it, called the Osteria.

A heavy artillery fire from Eugene's side opened the battle. Then the infantry fell in line, taking the Osteria in a quick assault and endeavoring to close the sluices of the canals. Just as they were occupied with this difficult and to them puzzling piece of work, the imperial troops were surprised by a vigorous attack of the French regiments, by which they were driven back and the Osteria taken from them. The Austrians again captured the bridge and building, but were obliged to give them up again and again. At the head of his men Eugene stormed the position for the third time, drove the enemy's ranks into the river, and prepared to take the intrenchments. But he was received with a heavy grenade fire which swept away whole lines, so that he was obliged to retire again.

In the meantime the Duke of Vendôme appeared on the battle-field with fresh troops. It was Prince Leopold who bore the first shock of their attack. His soldiers had waded through the canals in order to reach the enemy the sooner, and had attacked them with their bayonets. But they were met by such a murderous hail of bullets, great and small, that the Prussians were obliged to withdraw. It was only for a short time, however, just long enough to take breath; for Dessau was not the man to be so quickly repulsed. "He is a cowardly dog who deserts his general!" he cried in a voice of thunder, and was the first to plunge again into the canal, followed by his grenadiers. Thus they victoriously advanced and passed through two canals, and were getting nearer and nearer to the foe, when for the second time they were driven back by the furious fire of the French cannon and rifles; and late in the afternoon they took refuge with Eugene's exhausted troops in a secure camp.

It was at Cassano that the "Dessau March" originated, a piece of music which was composed in honor of Leopold, and which still enjoys great popularity.

The day at Cassano was a disastrous one for the Germans, for more than a fifth of their army lay dead or wounded on the battle-field. For a long time Eugene was obliged to play at hide and seek with the enemy, being now too weak to engage in open warfare. But wherever he could injure the French, we may be sure he did so. Eugene's bloody partisan warfare is remembered to this day in Lombardy.

But in Paris they were evidently not quite satisfied with the operations of the firm "Vendôme brothers." Both of them were recalled and Duke Philip of Orleans and Marshal Marsin intrusted with the command of the army. This spurred Eugene on to measure his strength with these new representatives. Turin was the last refuge of Duke Victor Amadeus of Savoy; this time-server had been thus driven to extremity. Starhemberg held the city with seven thousand men. A French army forty thousand strong now appeared to besiege it. But Eugene arrived on the ground before them. He crossed the Po with thirty thousand men, passed around the French intrenchments, crossed the Dora also, and went into camp between this river and the Stura.

At daybreak on the seventh of September, 1706, the troops of the allied armies broke camp. They were divided into eight columns, of which four formed the first and four the second division. Scarcely had the French commanders noted Eugene's plan when they sent large reinforcements to the threatened spot and began a heavy cannonading. Of course the imperial batteries did not remain silent. This artillery battle thundered for more than two hours. Meanwhile, in Turin, Count von Daun was making ready with twelve battalions, four hundred grenadiers, five hundred cavalrymen, and six fieldpieces for a timely sortie. The inhabitants of Turin witnessed the progress of the battle from the walls and the roofs of the houses and churches, praying devoutly for the success of the German arms.

The Prussian troops had scarcely come up when they were ordered to attack. Prince Leopold at their head, they advanced upon the enemy as though they were on the parade-ground, with erect, firm bearing and without firing a shot. A terrific fire greeted them; the enemies' bullets swept them in front and in the flank, and although they answered with a very rapid battalion fire, the battle was too unequal and they were obliged to retire. As soon as Eugene noticed this he hurried to the spot, to the support of the brave Prussian regiments, with the remainder of the left wing, which was soon followed by the centre and the right wing. The fighting broke out all along the long line of battle. Both sides fought recklessly, neither advancing, but on the other hand neither giving way.

Eugene's attention was centred on the Prussians; the Prince of Dessau, his valiant ally of Höchstädt and Cassano, seemed to him the right man to strike a tremendous blow. It needed but a few words. Leopold, the "bull-dog," as Eugene is said to have called him, threw himself with his already much decimated battalions with terrific fury upon the enemy's intrenchments. Nothing intimidated the faithful fellows, nothing could stop them. They crossed the moat, took the redoubts, and intrenched themselves therein. Eugene was in the midst of them. His horse was shot under him and he fell to the ground. The terror of death was upon him. But no!— immediately he arose and hurried on, at the head of his men.

Simultaneously with this brilliant success, the Prince of Württemberg penetrated the intrenchments from the opposite side. Eugene's positive orders were that the left wing should occupy the intrenchments which had been taken until the right wing and the centre had also taken the intrenchments. But alas! in the enthusiasm of victory the left wing hurried after their advancing brothers, and the fortifications remained unprotected. But Eugene was watching the progress of the battle. Starhemberg's regiment was called upon, occupied the fortifications, turned the captured French cannon about and shelled the fleeing enemy with them. The French at the centre fought just as doggedly. There Philip of Orleans and Marsin were in command. Three times the intrenchments were taken by the allies; three times they were recaptured by the French, until, at last, the Duke of Savoy took them for the fourth time—and held them.

Thus the French were repulsed at all points. In great disorder they hurried toward the Po and the Dora. It was now the faithful Daun's turn. He received them, not with open arms, but with powder and lead instead, took part of them prisoners and drove the rest into the cold waters of the river, to cool the heat of their flight.

Thus the rule of the French in Milan was overthrown. Amidst the boundless rejoicings of the delivered city, Eugene made his entry into it, as its imperial governor. From this time the plans of Louis the Fourteenth were frustrated. He must have been sick enough with rage at the little *abbé*, for the pills he had had to swallow in Italy were bitter as gall. And still the triumphs of Germany over the French were not complete. While a small imperial force marched straight to Naples to harass the French there, Eugene and Victor Amadeus made ready to carry the war into Southern France. After an extremely arduous march over the Alps, they reached Valette, which lies about a half-hour's march from Toulon, and went into camp there. During the following days Toulon was shelled by the Austrians. Nothing more was done, however, as the French were gathering in ever increasing numbers; so Eugene wisely withdrew. The fall of Toulon was the dearest wish of the English and Hollanders, but Eugene preferred not to burn his fingers in their interests. Besides, from the standpoint of the soldier, his retreat through the enemy's country was a greater feat than the storming of Toulon would have been. On the road he casually took Susa; and he arrived again in Vienna in the Autumn of 1707, where he was greeted at court, as well as by the people, as the deliverer of Italy. He met with a brilliant and extremely friendly reception.

Chapter VIII
Malplaquet

The Duke of Marlborough had fought against France in the Netherlands in recent years, with more or less success. But latterly fortune had turned her back upon him; Ghent, Brussels, Bruges, and other fortified towns had again fallen into the hands of the French; for Marshal Vendôme and the Duke of Burgundy were very alert generals.

One of Marlborough's letters to Lord Godolphin shows how deeply he felt the hopelessness of his situation. He wrote: "As there is a God in heaven I put my trust in Him, for without Him our prospects are truly terrible." Eugene did not wish to desert the brave Duke in this great extremity. To be sure, money was scarce in Vienna; Hungary and Siebenbürgen could contribute nothing, the impoverished hereditary lands were just as unable to furnish sufficient ready money, and loans were to be had only at exorbitant rates. In addition, there was a split in the parties at court. They were weary of war, and one interfered with another's counsels and plans. It was almost a miracle that it was possible for Eugene to impose his plans for war upon the Council, and to organize a well-trained army in the shortest possible time. It was, no doubt, Marlborough's messengers of distress, and his own extreme sense of duty urging him not to desert his faithful brother-in-arms, which conquered all obstacles.

With indefatigable haste Eugene set out with his army, crossed the Moselle on the twenty-eighth of June, 1708, and joined the cavalry on the third of July at Düren. A few days later his army and Marlborough's were united. This was help in time of need. The first meeting of the two generals was touching. Marlborough embraced Eugene and called him his saviour. The noble Savoyard directed his friend to trust in God. "With His help," said he, "even though I pay the penalty with my life, I shall obtain satisfaction."

Eugene next hurried to Brussels, which the French had again given up, into the arms of his mother, whom he had not seen since she was driven from France. What must have been the feelings of mother and son? Eugene had taken vengeance on their deadly enemy for her and the whole family of Soissons, and had punished and humiliated him. He had already twice entered France at the head of a victorious army, he had been successful in the Netherlands, and the road to Paris was open to him. Full of happiness and enthusiasm the mother parted from her heroic son. And soon new tidings of victory arrived to gladden the lonely widow. The aged woman passed away on the arrival of the news of the victory of Malplaquet (1709). She died happy, for her beloved son had avenged her husband and herself.

Marlborough and Eugene with eighty thousand men came upon the enemy at Oudenarde. The French leaders disagreed as thoroughly among themselves as the allies were united. They had forgotten to protect the bridges over the Scheldt. The allies used five of these and on the eleventh of July, 1708, crossed the river; as they arrived they placed themselves according to battalions in battle array.

How easily the French might have prevented this and have attacked the separated little companies and conquered them! They chose quite different tactics—they hastily intrenched themselves. It was the English Colonel Cadogan who first dealt with the enemy. He easily overthrew the twenty squadrons opposed to him, scattered four battalions of infantry, and in doing so he frightened three others so thoroughly that they ran away without firing a shot.

That was a merry introduction, but the real drama was to follow. Marlborough now advanced with the principal strength of the army. The French defended themselves with the utmost bravery; and as they were much more numerous, they forced the English back. But Marlborough was of a tenacious character. With all his might he again pressed forward, not only reconquering the lost ground, but continually advancing. Eugene knew how to gain successes of the same sort. The allies bore down ever more heavily upon the French. The battle became disorganized and ended in a series of bloody hand-to-hand skirmishes. But the English and Germans understood this kind of fighting also, for they had learned it under the murderous fire at Höchstädt.

Toward evening the Hollanders received orders to march round the French right wing, a task that they accomplished with remarkable quickness and precision. The allies then pressed forward in a great half-circle and overthrew the enemy. Seven of the enemy's cavalry regiments were cut down, and Vendôme's battalions of the guard, led by himself, were shattered by the iron knights of England. At sunset the day had been gloriously won; a victory like that of Höchstädt. Vendôme fled to Ghent, and there remained three days in bed to sleep off his chagrin.

After the battle of Oudenarde the allied armies remained in the Netherlands. In Eugene's own words, it was now time "to profit honestly by the victory."

In order to accomplish this it was necessary to take a fortified place, and Lille or Ryssel seemed to Eugene the most appropriate. He was not a waverer or one who would discard to-morrow the plans of yesterday; and in this Marlborough was his faithful colleague. Then quickly to work! The allies shelled the fortress of Lille daily with a hundred and twenty cannon, eighty mortars, and twenty howitzers. This must certainly have helped matters. Marshal Vendôme's fingers were itching to relieve Lille, which Marlborough with his seventy thousand men prevented, holding the Marshal at a good distance, so that Eugene could operate with freedom against the fortifications. At last the Austrians had opened a breach. Eugene was quickly on the ground. One night he advanced to the breach with the storming columns, but was very unlucky. The enemy must have learned of his design; they received the advancing columns with a murderous fire of grapeshot and also set off two powder-mines with horrible results. Of course the Austrians were obliged to retreat.

But postponement is not abandonment; and the maxim, "A burnt child shuns the fire," did not apply to Eugene. One night he was again before the breach. All was ready for the onslaught. The roll of the drums and the calls of horns and trumpets were kindling the Austrians with enthusiasm, but it was a difficult piece of work. Three times they were beaten back, but the fourth time they were successful. Several outposts were taken and occupied. During this attack Eugene was slightly wounded on the head. He transferred the command to Marlborough, knowing it to be in good hands.

About this time Eugene received, among other letters, one which on opening he found to contain a piece of blank paper which had been soaked in some greasy, sticky stuff. Eugene dropped the paper and said: "It is not the first of its kind which I have received." Of course the paper was poisoned. It was bound about the neck of a dog, and after a few hours the animal died.

But let us return to the siege of Lille. On the third of October the grand attack was made. Both sides fought with admirable courage. Eugene, as well as Bouffleurs, gave his men an example worthy of emulation; both fought in the front ranks. Eugene was wounded and fell to the ground. His men raised a shout of horror. "It is nothing!" he cried, covered the wound with his handkerchief and pressed forward. It was with great difficulty that his friends could persuade him to leave the battle-field while the assault was proceeding. A terrible slaughter began. The Frenchmen defended every inch of ground with heroic courage. The men fought with bayonets; they strangled one another with their hands; and all the time the heavy artillery of the besiegers was thundering and was opening new breaches here and there. Where the moats were not filled with wounded or dead bodies, they were piled up with bits of sod, gabions, and bundles of faggots to make them passable. At last Bouffleurs lost all hope of holding the city. Fighting, he retired into the citadel, which, after a defence of two months, he at last also surrendered to the allies.

Without reading the conditions of surrender, Eugene signed the paper with the words: "Marshal Bouffleurs cannot demand anything which I shall not be able to grant!" Nobly spoken, valiant Knight!

When they wished to give grand *fêtes* at The Hague in honor of the Prince, he begged them rather to give the large sums of money which would have been expended to the faithful Dutch soldiers who had been invalided at the defence of Lille. Eugene had the gratifying consciousness of having also freed Flanders from the French by his prompt interference. In the following words he shows what importance he attributed to the campaign of 1708: "He who was not in it has never experienced anything."

The peace negotiations at The Hague between the warring powers came to nothing. After the last great victories Eugene was able to press his claims in the name of his Emperor (Joseph the First). He demanded the whole undivided Spanish inheritance, also Alsace and Sundgau, the bishoprics of Metz, Toul, and Verdun, which had formerly been unjustly taken from the German empire. After a long period of weakness in state and international affairs, this was once more a virile German demand. The Marquis de Lorcy, a suave French courtier, the representative of Louis the Fourteenth at The Hague, opened his eyes very wide and begged leave to communicate this demand to the King. As was anticipated, Louis declined the terms of peace. The storms of war began anew to discharge their fury upon the frightened nations. The Germans, together with the English and Dutch, were once more quickly in the field. Every one felt that the new campaign would be a very sanguinary one. The injured vanity of the French King demanded atonement, revenge.

Against about one hundred thousand allies, Louis put one hundred and twenty thousand men in the field. Villars, with whom we became acquainted during the Italian campaign, made great promises to the Parisians. The first task was to take the fortress of Tournay from the French. This was successful. The next was to arrive at Mons before the French. It was also accomplished. This was Villar's *début*, and the King of France was not greatly pleased. He sent the brave Bouffleurs after him to urge him on, for his confidence in Villars was still unshaken. Besides, Bouffleurs did not come alone, but brought with him a valiant troop. The gay Marshal was much elated; and was quite confident of victory. And with him the whole French army rejoiced, convinced that they should strike the Germans a deadly blow and then themselves dictate the terms of peace.

While the French gave themselves up to these undue rejoicings, Eugene and Marlborough were composedly making all arrangements to wreck the Marshal's plan and spoil his fun. They quickly set out with ninety thousand men and occupied all the highways, in order to prevent the enemy from reaching Mons.

Mons lies in the province of Hainaut. This region is hilly for the most part, cut up by gorges and little streams, and covered thickly with timber. In front of Marlborough's position lay the forest of Lanière; in front of Eugene's, the forest of Taisnière. The corner which juts out toward the north is called the forest of Sart. Between the above-mentioned forests lie Aulnoit and the Wolf's Cave. The first was occupied by Marlborough, and the last by Eugene; between them was a series of more or less deep ravines. It was in no respect a well-selected position; it was taken only because it was necessary to put themselves quickly on the defensive against a threatened attack of the enemy.

Villars's centre stood upon the clearing of Aulnoit, his wings were covered by the above-mentioned forests. Besides this he had intrenchments thrown up in haste and barricades constructed. He must have been somewhat nervous. The allied generals observed the enemy's position from the windmill at Sart. Their plan was to engage the attention of the enemy's centre by a feigned attack, while they really were trying to throw the left wing from its position. Between Marlborough and Eugene, eighteen battalions of imperial infantry were posted.

In the early hours of a cold, wet, September morning, the ninth, the allied armies quietly gathered under their standards, while the Frenchmen, on the other hand, being confident of an easy victory, were cheering continuously for their King and for Marshal Villars. As usual the thunder of the cannon opened the battle. Amidst their brazen clangor, the Saxons under Schulenberg pressed forward on the edge of the forest of Sart to within pistol-shot of the enemy. But there the valiant Albergotti opened such a heavy musketry fire on them that the battalions at the front fell back panic-stricken and were stopped only by those behind them. United they pushed forward once more, Eugene leading them. The first redoubt was taken by storm, and soon afterwards the second also was taken. Eugene's infantry followed eagerly in the victorious path of their advancing comrades, but were soon retarded by a thick growth of bushes and trees. The battalions were separated and at last became thoroughly disordered. The worst of it was, that they came upon a fresh barricade of logs. But great as the difficulties were, they were conquered at last; the forest of Sart was taken, and the French driven out of it.

While these events were taking place in Eugene's division, the Prussian General von Lottum, of Marlborough's division, with twenty-two battalions, made a daring attack on the principal front of the French left wing, where Villars himself commanded. Although whole ranks of the faithful grenadiers fell before the enemy's grapeshot and musketry hail, they worked their way forward with astonishing endurance and had the pleasure of seeing Villars retreating behind the forest.

While he was busy re-forming his line of battle he was surprised by the Prince of Orange with thirty battalions. A fierce fight ensued. The French defended themselves heroically and repulsed their assailants. But not for long; for Eugene came to the rescue. On horseback he reduced the wild confusion of the battle, encouraging here, praising there, or consoling. Once more he was wounded by a musket ball, in the back of his head. He had no time to have the wound dressed. To his remonstrating friends he smilingly said: "If I should die, the bandage would do me no good, and if I live, the surgeon can do his work this evening." Thus he plunged again into the fury of the battle. And still there was no decisive victory although Marlborough's and Eugene's troops fought so bravely. But the heroic Prince's eye is alert and is watching, in spite of great loss of blood and intense pain from the wound in his head.

At last the decisive moment came. Hazarding a last tremendous blow, for his troops were exhausted by the long struggle, Villars sent thirty battalions with lowered bayonets against Eugene. In order to do this he had drawn a large part of the infantry from the redoubts on his right, which Bouffleurs until now had defended so heroically. Eugene immediately espied the vulnerable point and, gathering his infantry together, he dashed upon the much weakened left wing of the foe. Here another terrible struggle took place. But all their bravery and heroic devotion availed the French nothing. At the head of his men Eugene broke through their centre. His men were not to be held back any longer. Starhemberg's cavalry rode and cut down everything that resisted them; the platoon fire of several Prussian battalions likewise did terrible destruction. The French fled.

PRINCE EUGENE
before the battle of Malplaquet

The other wing of the allies was equally fortunate. Excited by the victorious shouts of the Germans, the English were not left behind. With fifteen battalions supported by seventeen squadrons under Bülow, Orkney took the intrenchments at Bleron. The Prince of Orange, the hero of the day, again took an important part in the battle; and although an extremely fierce cavalry skirmish ensued upon the plain of Malplaquet and the Frenchmen enjoyed a few victorious moments, the imperial cavalry from the other wing, appearing like a stormcloud on the field of battle, overwhelmed the enemy with tremendous force. They gave way and fled. Unfortunately, the allies were too exhausted to pursue them effectually. Only twelve squadrons of the imperial cavalry harassed them on their retreat, which was conducted skilfully by Bouffleurs.

The battle of Malplaquet, as the fight over the French intrenchments was called, was one of the fiercest of the War of the Spanish Succession. The loss on both sides in dead and wounded was about the same, probably about thirty-six thousand men. The great battle-field was horrible to look upon. Where the Dutch battalions of the guard had stood, the corpses lay in ranks before the intrenchments, most of them stripped of their clothes and horribly mutilated. The moats were filled to the top with dead bodies. The allied victors spent the night upon the battle-field. What a night! as terrible as the day had been!

The battle of Malplaquet was the last in the long and extremely bloody War of the Spanish Succession, excepting several clever operations against the French, and minor encounters. For a long time the discussions over "mine" and "thine" continued. The French were scarcely able to resign themselves, but at last, after negotiations between the several States, in February, 1714, peace was made between the Emperor Charles the Sixth (Joseph the First had died in 1711) and King Louis the Fourteenth of France at Rastadt. This was for the most part Eugene's work; and his opponent at the green table was Marshal Villars. Eugene raised his voice powerfully in Germany's interest; Germany was indebted to him for whatever he succeeded in obtaining under many unfortunate and unfavorable circumstances. France kept Landau, but resigned the other territories which she had conquered; Milan, Naples, Sardinia, and the Spanish Netherlands passed to the Emperor.

Villars and Eugene parted friends at Rastadt. They had learned to respect one another. At their farewell Villars uttered these parting words: "Your foes are not in the enemy's camp, but in Vienna, as mine are in Versailles." This was a prophecy which was later to be fulfilled in a terrible manner.

Chapter IX
Eugene at Belgrade

After a few years of peace we see Eugene again taking up his sword against the Turks. The Venetians needed assistance against the Sublime Porte. At first it was thought that all difficulties could be settled by the pen, but the gentlemen in Constantinople assumed such an arrogant tone that it was impossible for Vienna to countenance it. Besides, the imperial house was much more powerful than in former days, when the Turks had advanced to the very gates of Vienna. Having vanquished the French, Austria was confident that she could conquer the Turks also. But the latter thought otherwise and were determined to regain what they had lost, at all costs. We shall see what happened.

Appointed imperial Governor-General of the Netherlands—no slight proof of the boundless confidence of his Emperor and master—Prince Eugene of Savoy prepared for a valiant defence against the grimmest foe of Christendom.

Surrounded by a group of heroes, including the daring Heister (called "the scourge of the Turks"), the excellent cavalry commander Palffy, Prince Alexander of Württemberg, the faithful Mercy, the expert soldier Starhemberg, and others, he left Vienna in order to join the army which was gathering at Peterwardein, in the Summer of 1716.

The Turks meanwhile had not been dilatory. Their army, numbering at least two hundred thousand men, was, according to Turkish standards, well fitted out and amply furnished with all requisites. Relying upon this, the Grand Vizier Ali wrote to the Field-Marshal General, Prince Eugene, among other things, these words: "The Ottoman Empire expects to win much glory and many victories in this campaign, whereas your shameful conduct will bring, not only upon you, but upon your children and grandchildren, misfortunes and curses and a shameful defeat." The Turks put on an air of innocence, but everyone knew just what to expect from them.

It was not long before the two armies were standing face to face, for both sides appeared to be in great haste. Field-Marshal Palffy, with a small body of men, hazarded a bold ride in order to reconnoitre the enemy's position. Their expedition led them through ravines and ditches and demanded a great deal of courage. Suddenly twenty thousand Turkish horsemen fell upon Palffy's company of scarcely two thousand men. In this rough country retreat and advance were equally dangerous; it was a desperate situation. But their gallant leader did not lose his head. He and his men defended themselves bravely and the enemy were badly worsted in spite of their advantage in numbers; and Palffy got safely back to Eugene. It now seemed as though the Turks were preparing to besiege Peterwardein. They dug trenches, threw up earthworks, erected redoubts, and continually shelled Eugene's position.

He was not the man to put up quietly with these annoyances for any length of time. His plan was to attack the enemy before they had become established in their new position or had seized the means for an energetic defence. With his characteristic rapidity Eugene made all his arrangements for an attack. The fourth of August was to be the decisive day. The Turks must have noticed that something was about to happen. They were stirring very early; and as it grew lighter, one could see hill and valley covered with the countless ranks of their hosts.

At seven o'clock in the morning, Eugene's left wing commenced the attack. Prince Alexander of Württemberg led the first storming column. Without meeting with any particular resistance he took one of the enemy's batteries, while the imperial cavalry, which followed his infantry, put the Turkish horsemen to flight. The troops were overjoyed at this; but the hardest work was still to come. Simultaneously with this attack, the imperial infantry, which was occupying the other intrenchments, was to advance on the enemy. In the narrow passages of the earthworks this manœuvre was not executed with the expected precision. It took longer to form the ranks outside the intrenchments than had been expected. Taking advantage of this, the Turks threw themselves on the advancing enemy in overpowering numbers. With fierce cries they drove them back, pushing forward with them into the first and second lines of intrenchments, but were quickly driven out again by the imperial cavalry, which came dashing up.

The infantry re-formed their ranks and again rapidly advanced. There was another terrific encounter. The imperial cuirassiers held the advantage; whatever came within reach was cut down by their terrific blows. The light Turkish cavalry were scattered like spray before the wind. However, they still fought with iron endurance and were even successful here and there. One section of the imperial infantry was repulsed again and again. The Turks, with loud cries of victory, began the pursuit in the heat of the fight; but in doing so exposed both of their flanks.

This was the moment for Eugene to strike a decisive blow. With the rapidity of lightning he threw Heister's cavalry on the left wing of the enemy. The battalions of the Prince of Württemberg attacked them on the right and in the centre; the scattered columns were re-forming for a new and victorious assault. Attacked from three sides at once with great fury, shelled by the cannon from the walls of Peterwardein, succumbing in bloody bayonet fights with their antagonists, and overthrown in a hand-to-hand struggle with the more powerful German soldiers, the Turks turned for a hurried flight. After them in furious haste stormed the German cavalry. Whole regiments were cut down and others taken prisoners. The Germans assaulted the last stronghold of the Turks, their wagon-barricade: further resistance was useless.

While the imperial commander Prince Eugene, on horseback and exposed to all the hardships and dangers of the fight, had been directing the battle, the Grand Vizier Ali had not for a moment left his tent, where he had been standing immovable beside the sacred banner of the Prophet. The flight of his troops at last aroused him. With his naked sabre he went to meet the fleeing men and cut down several of them. He implored, he commanded, he cursed them. All in vain. The current of flight and defeat was not to be stemmed. He then placed himself at the head of his bodyguard, plunged into the tide of battle, and soon fell mortally wounded. His defeated and disorganized army hastened on to Belgrade. Temesvar was taken by the Austrians. Eugene had occasion once more to hold a thanksgiving service on the field of battle.

Eugene's victory at Peterwardein caused great enthusiasm throughout the whole of Europe. The Savoyard was the fêted hero of young and old, aristocrat and humble citizen. While the blessings of the whole German people were following him on his path of victory, the monarchs of Europe were vying with one another in offering him tokens of their admiration and gratitude. The Pope presented him with a consecrated hat and sword, and Marshal Villars honored the famous hero of Peterwardein with a personal letter.

Although the defeat of the Turks had been so complete and so terrible, they could not rest until they tried their luck in a second campaign. The whole of Europe rejoiced over this news, not doubting that the old arch-enemy of Christendom would now receive his death-blow. Young nobles and the chief princes flocked to the imperial standards in order to join in the fight against the Turks and to study the art of war under Eugene's leadership. As usual, he was now prompt and ready. On the ninth of June, 1717, he set out from Peterwardein; on the fourteenth he was at Pancsova; and on the fifteenth and sixteenth the imperial army crossed the Danube. He purposed no less a feat than "to reconquer for the Emperor" the fortress of Belgrade, which was garrisoned by thirty thousand picked Turkish troops. This was an extremely hazardous undertaking, for two hundred thousand Turks under command of the Grand Vizier Chalis of Adrianople were already on their way to interfere with his plans. But in spite of this, the Christian army was in good spirits, and their confidence was absolute in their general, who was bold, as well as gifted, and seasoned in battle.

This occasion again brought into play all the resources of Eugene's genius. He had to prepare for defence in two directions: first, against a sortie of the garrison; and secondly, against an attack from the Turkish army of relief. For this purpose he protected his camp by quickly constructed fort-like walls, deep, wide trenches, earthworks, and rifle-pits. At the same time he caused exits to be made in the principal wall here and there, so that in case of danger from the outside, his men would be able to reach the open field quickly. He bridged over the morasses, caused the sconce of the Semlin bridge on the Banat side of the Danube to be garrisoned, the island in the Danube at Belgrade to be protected by redoubts—in short he did everything that forethought and care could suggest to hold off and if possible to crush an enemy possessing three times his strength.

In the midst of these extensive preparations for the battle Eugene was surprised by a fearful natural catastrophe. A mighty hurricane broke loose, tearing the heavy iron chains that bound the ships, as though they had been hempen ropes, destroying the bridges which had been constructed, and dashing the Austrian and Turkish vessels lying in the Danube into a confused heap. Taking advantage of this disturbance, ten thousand Turks crossed the Save to take the Austrian intrenchments. An unexampled confusion took possession of the Germans; but a Hessian captain, quickly gathering together his half company, threw himself against the numerous advancing foes. He had the courage and good fortune to be able to hold his ground until two grenadier companies hurried to the scene and drove back the enemy. While this event was taking place, the janissaries had fixed their attention upon the Austrian intrenchments. With resounding cries to Allah they were soon inside, massacring the bewildered Austrian soldiers, but were as quickly surprised by two hundred and fifty cuirassiers, who came dashing up to ride them down or drive them into the angry waters of the Danube. At the same time the imperial batteries opened a murderous fire on Belgrade. Large sections of the fortifications were levelled to the ground, and the water-front of the city was laid in ruins. Then the news was brought to Prince Eugene that Chalis was approaching with reinforcements. At first, merely a rumor to which little credence was given, it soon turned out to be a fact. Hussars and Servians began to arrive at the fortifications, which had already been occupied by their forerunners, the light Turkish Cavalry skirmishers.

A few days later, Eugene had the foe before and behind him. Shelled from all sides, Eugene needed great coolness. Thousands would have lost their heads in such a situation. His resolution was taken. While a very small part of his army kept guard over Belgrade, with the remaining forty thousand men he boldly challenged the Grand Vizier Chalis. Eugene's situation at Belgrade recalls in many respects that of Werder at Belfort. The infantry formed the centre, the cavalry was posted on the wings. No one could deceive himself as to the seriousness of the situation. There were but two courses open; to conquer, or to die! And in a council of war Eugene said plainly enough: "Either I shall gain possession of Belgrade or the Turks will take me."

The officers were commanded to give their orders coolly and quietly, without shouting or showing impatience. Neither officer nor soldier was allowed to leave his appointed place, and no one on pain of death should seek for spoils or plunder. Lastly, the soldiers were reminded that they had to do with Turks, Tartars, and enemies of that sort, from whom there was little to fear if they were met with due coolness and firmness. Shortly after midnight the regiments moved out of the intrenchments to place themselves in battle array.

It was a cold, clear night in August, so the Turks could observe the marching of the troops. It was not until nearly daylight that a fog covered the landscape, so dense that the nearest objects could not be distinguished. Enveloped in this gray veil the Austrians advanced on the Turkish fortifications. The fog was now so thick that in spite of all precautions Palffy's cavalry lost their way. As the infantry had orders to follow the cavalry, they also got too far to the right. In this way an empty space was left in the centre, which the Turks immediately filled out with several battalions, so that they were in the midst of the Austrian position.

Thus the battle began; and soon the whole right wing was involved in a bitter fight. Palffy's cavalry were worthy of all honor; every one of them fought like a hero, but against such overwhelming numbers their destruction was certain. It was General von Mercy who hurried to the relief of his brothers-in-arms; the gallant Starhemberg also, with his infantry, was not behindhand. With irresistible energy the battalions attacked the enemy at the front, and the cavalry fell upon his flank. Such an onslaught could not be sustained for any length of time. The Turks fled, leaving their batteries in the hands of the Austrians.

PRINCE EUGENE
at Belgrade

During this fighting on the right wing, the battle broke out gradually along the whole line. The fog had become still denser and more impenetrable. Both sides fired without being able to see one another. In slow marching order the Austrian infantry moved forward. Coming upon the Turkish trenches they took them quickly by storm and crossed over upon the corpses of their foes.

In other parts of the great battle-field the Turks were gaining the advantage. A large body of their troops, led astray by the fog, found itself again between the two separated wings of the Austrians. That meant some desperate fighting. Toward eight o'clock in the morning a light breeze at last scattered the mists which, until now, had hidden the battle-field.

A single glance over the confused panorama showed Eugene the fearful danger in which he stood. It was such moments as these, however, which demonstrated his greatness. With him decision and execution were one. The enemy must not be allowed to make use of their advantage. Prince von Bevern received orders to throw himself impetuously upon them with the second division; Eugene at the head of the united cavalry regiments stormed their flanks. The Turks defended themselves lustily, especially as they had now discovered, too late, their favorable position. There was no power to resist the tremendous onslaught of the Austrians, the Turks wavered, gave way; the battle line was once more established. And now the drums rolled, the horns pealed forth, and the flags waved aloft—the signal for a general attack on the Turkish camp all along the line.

There were many bleeding heads; there was no holding back on either side; they surged back and forth. Only one Turkish battery upon a hill was holding its own. From its eighteen cannon it poured forth death and destruction upon the advancing Austrians. This must be taken and silenced. Ten companies of grenadiers and four battalions whose wings were covered by squadrons of cavalry were assigned the task of taking the battery by storm. With flying banners and bands playing, marching close together, shoulder to shoulder as compact as a wall, the brave fellows pressed forward. They were met by a terrific fire, which tore deep gaps in their ranks. Regardless of their falling comrades, passing over their wounded and dead bodies, they pressed onward with loud cries of victory, and reached the top. Without firing a shot, with lowered bayonets they charged the enemy (mostly janissaries) like a stormcloud, until all were cut down and the battery was taken.

It was exactly nine o'clock in the morning when the enemy left their fortified camp in great haste. The gradually decreasing thunder of the Austrian cannon accompanied them, but the light cavalry pursued the defeated Turks. It was a great battle and a great victory! The Turks lost about twenty thousand men, while Eugene's loss was but fifteen hundred. The trophies of war included nearly two hundred cannon, one hundred and fifty flags, and nine horsetails, not forgetting the captured treasure in the deserted Turkish camp, consisting of bejewelled weapons and other articles of luxury.

Eugene sent General Count Hamilton at once with news of the victory to the Emperor, Charles the Sixth. The anxious suspense of all minds had been so great on account of Eugene's dangerous situation that the rejoicings were unbounded. As Count Hamilton, according to the custom of that time, after having delivered his message to the Emperor, accompanied by the pealing tones of the six postillions of "the Favorite" who rode before him, passed through the Kärnthner gate into the city, across the moat and by way of the Kohlmarkt to the Castle, the crowds were so great that the carriage could scarcely make its way through them. A few days later, Colonel Count Rabutin brought the news that Belgrade also had surrendered. Nearly six hundred cannon, the whole flotilla on the Danube, and a great deal of ammunition fell into the hands of the victors.

One year later, after the Turks had been defeated in several more small skirmishes and battles, Prince Eugene made peace with them, in the name of the Emperor, at Passarowitz. Banat, Slavonia, a part of Bosnia, Servia, and Wallachia passed over to Austria, not forgetting Hungary, which had been conquered before this. The strangest part of the affair was, that even the Turkish Sultan could not abstain from showing Eugene how highly he esteemed him. The Turkish ambassador was instructed to present the Prince with two Arabian horses, a costly sword, and a turban. At the same time he accompanied the presents with the explanation: "The sabre is the symbol of your valor; the others are for your keen wit, your wise counsel, and wiser execution."

Chapter X
Last Days

After a peaceful interval of sixteen years, during which Eugene had devoted himself to the study of the arts and sciences, he was obliged once more to take up his sword. France was again menacing the peace of Europe. She was not willing that the Elector of Saxony should become King of Poland, but presented another candidate and seized this opportunity of picking a quarrel with Austria and Germany. Eugene therefore found himself promptly seated in the saddle once more, ready to show the King of France (now Louis the Fifteenth) that he still understood his profession. Unfortunately this war was begun and conducted in a very sleepy fashion, so that Eugene had only twenty thousand men to oppose the one hundred and twenty thousand Frenchmen, instead of the imposing army originally promised him by the Emperor; and even though this small number was gradually doubled by accessions of Prussians and other troops of the empire, it was not possible to undertake anything important with them. In spite of this Eugene manœuvred so cleverly with his little army that in a two-years' campaign (1734-1735) France gained no great advantage on the Rhine and took possession only of Philippsburg.

As things stood—the Emperor without money, the army unpaid and without bread—it was almost a miracle that France did not gain more advantages. It was Eugene, the conqueror at Zenta, Höchstädt, Turin, Oudenarde, Malplaquet, Peterwardein, and Belgrade who prevented it. In this war against France Eugene made the personal acquaintance of the Crown Prince of Prussia, later King Frederick the Great. Frederick greeted the noble Knight with the significant words: "I should like to be allowed to witness the manner in which a hero collects his laurels."

Eugene felt a real attachment for the Crown Prince. He regretted that he had not had the good fortune to become acquainted with him earlier, and said to him, "My Prince, everything about you convinces me that you will one day become a great military leader." Once when Frederick had cordially saluted the Duke of Württemberg, who was an old friend, Eugene turned to him with the words, "Will your Majesty not kiss my old cheek also?" a request with which Frederick immediately complied: a touching token of the hearty esteem in which the aspiring young hero held the old retiring one.

In the late Autumn of 1735 peace was made. The Emperor Charles the Sixth suffered the loss of some territory in Italy, but had the great satisfaction of seeing France recognize the Pragmatic Sanction (the right of accession of the female line of the house of Hapsburg). Peace! For the present only a short earthly peace; but the noble Knight was not far from the eternal rest. But we must touch upon other things before bringing this sketch to a close.

We have intentionally described Eugene in the character of a soldier and hero first, and have thus passed over many events of his life. Let us now return several years into the past; it will show us how even the best and greatest of men are subject to enmity and slander. The reader may remember Marshal Villars's remark at Rastadt: "Eugene's enemies are not in the French camp, but in Vienna." Probably Eugene did not let these words trouble him much at the time, for who is without enemies? The man is still to be born who is able to please everybody. But Villars's remark had a significance which Eugene was to understand better some years later.

In the last two campaigns against the Turks, Eugene had conferred the greatest glory on the Austrian arms. He was the most admired hero in the imperial army, and possessed the undisputed love and esteem of his Emperor and of the whole German people. Although all this gratified the noble-minded Prince, it did not make him proud or arrogant, as fools in such a situation are apt to be. On the contrary, he pursued the even tenor of his way, flattering no one, though flattery is quite customary and expected at court. War and a long life spent in the camp had lent his manner a certain bluntness. He never tried to conceal his meaning, and he spoke as he felt. This did not please many of the courtiers; they took it for granted that it bespoke a high opinion of his own merits. The wings of this proud eagle, they thought, who in eagle fashion aspired to mount to the sun, must be clipped.

As president of the Royal Council of War—the highest dignity in the state next to the Emperor—Prince Eugene had a great, if not the greatest influence in all business of state. Whatever he had once decided was right and good he would carry out, whether he was looked askance at for it or not. He urged the regulation of the finances, which, as we know, were in bad condition at that time in Austria. He demanded great economy in all affairs, and abolished a great many abuses. Among other things he procured a decree that no one should be allowed to buy his rank as an officer in the army, but that only those should be chosen who were really capable and worthy of the position. Next, he turned his attention to the corrupt practice of favoritism shown to distinguished relatives, which at that time was much in vogue in Vienna. He provided better care for the soldiers, but demanded also stricter discipline and subordination in the army. Of course this was a slap in the face for many. It was especially uncomfortable for the higher classes, where the greatest abuses had become habitual.

Now, the best cure was a radical one—to remove the noble Prince Eugene. But how? It was not very easy to overthrow such a man as this. The Spanish party at court understood the matter, however, and applied the lever at the right point; in other words, they began with the Emperor Charles the Sixth, who guarded his prerogatives anxiously and jealously. He could not endure that any one should presume to exercise any control over him even from a distance. So the Spaniards and Frenchmen whispered in his ear that Eugene was seeking to become a second Wallenstein; that the army was on his side; that it was most dangerous to give him freedom to carry out his ambitious plans.

Furthermore, Eugene was accused of expressing himself very openly on political questions in favor of Hungary, at the house of Countess Batthiany, a Hungarian. Others declared that he was jealous of the fame of his subordinates. They said that in order to test Guido Starhemberg's intrepidity he had caused bombs to be placed under the table before a banquet and had them exploded at the moment when Starhemberg was just about to propose the Emperor's health; and that Starhemberg was not at all disconcerted, but had coolly emptied his glass. Not content with this, they accused Eugene of having needlessly sacrificed a great many soldiers in the last war, and of having favored the cavalry at the expense of the infantry. In short, they found abundant matter for malicious attacks on him for his desperate situation at Belgrade where he had allowed himself to be surrounded by superior numbers. Of course they prudently failed to recall his brilliant victory.

All this had its effect; these malicious slanders succeeded in undermining the Emperor's confidence, which had appeared to be so absolute, and in a short time produced such a complete revolution in his sentiments for the Prince that he suddenly regarded his deeds and aspirations with changed eyes. Indeed, distrust and entire estrangement took the place of his former grateful regard. The men who encouraged this wicked calumny because they wished to ruin Eugene at all costs and drive him from the court were miserable tools of the Spanish court party, particularly of a certain Tedeschi, a spendthrift abbot, who played the clown and fun-maker at court, as well as the Count von Nimptsch, brother-in-law of the Emperor's favorite, Althan. Herr Althan himself and the Marquis von Thomas, the ambassador of Duke Victor Amadeus of Savoy, were also secretly concerned in this disgraceful affair. But the truth of the old maxim proved itself in this instance: "It is a long road which has no turning."

This treachery came to light through another's treachery. The valet of Count von Nimptsch, an enthusiastic admirer of the high-minded Prince Eugene, discovered the tricks of his master, possessed himself of written proofs of his treachery, took them to headquarters, and laid them before Prince Eugene.

What a surprise all this vileness was to the Prince! At first he could not and would not believe it. He could not imagine that the party had sunk so low. But there it was, black on white, it was a fact. His enemies had basely slandered him in order to accomplish his ruin.

Eugene did not hesitate a moment, but went straight to the Emperor, not in order to justify himself—for with his high character he did not feel it necessary—but to demand just punishment of the miserable slanderers. "Your Majesty," he said, "a pernicious plot has been concocted against me. Miserable slanderers have conspired against my honor and robbed me of the precious favor of my beloved Emperor. I demand satisfaction!" Eugene then revealed what had been done behind his back and named the dishonorable traitors openly. He could speak in plain terms, for a good conscience was his best weapon.

The Emperor was seized with the most painful embarrassment; he was silent with surprise—and shame.

But this did not satisfy Eugene. "I demand full satisfaction," said he firmly. "If this should be refused me, I shall be obliged to lay all my offices and honors at Your Majesty's feet. But I shall call upon all Europe to sit in judgment on the terrible injury which has been done me in case such an insult shall remain unpunished."

The Emperor tried to soothe the aggrieved hero, embraced him, and expressed the hope that they might still remain the same good old friends.

But this did not satisfy Eugene. He repeatedly demanded full satisfaction. He affirmed that the affair had gone too far for him to be put off with mere words, and that otherwise he must demand his dismissal.

The Emperor could not refuse. He gave Eugene his hand and ordered, in the first place, the arrest of Nimptsch and Tedeschi. A short time afterwards a special commission was assembled to conduct the investigation of the affair. It went forward very slowly, for the commissioners were loath to compromise people in high stations. During this time Eugene did not engage in any business of state, so that all public affairs came to a standstill. At last the head of the investigation commission, Count von Windischgrätz, made an end of the dilatory proceedings. He boldly informed the Emperor that it would be a perpetual disgrace to his Government if Prince Eugene, to whom the Austrian house owed eternal gratitude, should become the victim of a vile intrigue. He begged the Emperor to bring the guilty ones to justice and to carry out the sentence of the court without fear or favor. That was effective. The affair began to move rapidly. On the morning of the twelfth of December, 1719, the sentence of Tedeschi was read in front of the Corn Exchange, the Court House of that day, and was immediately executed. He was obliged to endure two hours in the pillory and received thirty heavy blows of the rod by the executioner. After this procedure he was driven in a cart outside the Kärnthner gate to the Tyrol road, where he was made to take an oath never to return to Austria. Count Nimptsch was taken in a closed carriage to Grätz, where he had to suffer two years' imprisonment, after which he was forever banished from Vienna. Althan escaped with a black eye, so to speak, and the Savoyan ambassador, Marquis von Thomas, might consider himself lucky in escaping the excited populace of Vienna unharmed.

This was the atonement which the Emperor Charles the Sixth made to Prince Eugene. After these events they became as good friends as they had formerly been, and the Emperor took every opportunity of showing by word and deed the warmest devotion to the Prince, as hundreds of personal letters from the Emperor to his faithful paladin testify. Eugene's health was of special concern to the Emperor, to show which a single document will suffice. A letter from the Emperor, dated November 27, 1729, ended with the very cordial words: "I implore you, my Prince, to take care of your health. Remember that we are growing older and not younger. Be careful of yourself, therefore, out of consideration for me, for I love you and embrace you heartily."

There remains nothing more to tell except of our hero's peculiarities of temperament, his manner of life, his character, and his death.

First of all we must defend Prince Eugene from the suspicion that he loved war. He regarded it as a necessary evil, but when it was no longer to be avoided he did not fear it. He did not hate the French and fight against them because the King had caused him and his family much sorrow and disgrace in his earliest youth, but because he considered them Germany's most bitter enemies, as they were continually seeking at all costs to injure her. He fought the Turks as the enemies of Christendom. He had so often seen the horrors of war which these barbarians had inflicted on the country and its people that it was no wonder he gladly battled with them and did everything in his power to deliver the civilized world from them.

Prince Eugene was a religious man, but did not parade his piety, as so many do. His modesty and humility, his untiring care for his soldiers, his beneficence and charity, were the outpouring of his religious nature. Eugene never let fall a word in praise of himself, and was always just to his subordinates and all his officers. It was also a trait of his noble character that he never censured deserving men. If, however, his duty made this necessary, he did it privately or in the presence of the Emperor, to whom he was accountable. He was a real father to his soldiers. He cared for them in every possible way, visiting the sick and wounded, and comforting the dying. It was no wonder that they were devoted to him.

He exercised an almost magical influence over them, which we must the more admire, because Prince Eugene was lacking in all the externals which usually make the deepest impression on people of the lower classes and on great masses. For, as we already know, he was small and insignificant-looking; besides, he did not understand the German language any too well, and was lacking in the eloquence which inflames the soldier to deeds of valor and inspires him to hasten recklessly into danger. But his affability and impartiality, his personal courage and the abandon with which he would place himself at the head of a storming column, sharing discomfort, want, misery, heat, and cold with his soldiers, compensated for the lack of external beauty. Under his leadership the troops felt themselves to be invincible. To use an old phrase: under him they would have undertaken to drive the devil out of hell.

At the same time Eugene had extremely clear judgment, not only amid the wild confusion of battle, where, as we have read, this quality very often inclined the victory to his side by means of prompt and energetic action, but also in his many other offices and affairs of state. He was always wise in the choice of his co-workers, gave them his full confidence, and scarcely ever was disappointed or deceived by one of them. As we have said, Eugene did not understand the German language well, and could scarcely write it at all. He always signed German reports or ordinances: "Eugenio von Savoy." This has been explained as follows: Eugene wished to indicate his extraction by the Italian word "Eugenio," his adopted fatherland by the German "von," and his birthland by the French "Savoy." However that may be, it is certain that Eugene devoted himself heart and soul to Germany and to the imperial house to the end of his days. He never forgot that, as an unknown and virtually banished youth, he had found a friendly and hospitable reception on German soil. Eugene's life was a perpetual expression of gratitude for this; and to Austria in particular he rendered imperishable services.

It is historic fact that not only the Emperor Charles the Sixth, but other competent judges, have acknowledged these services. King Frederick the Second of Prussia believed that the reign of Charles the Sixth closed much less brilliantly than it had begun, because of the death of Prince Eugene. Some years later, when that Prussian ruler declared war against Austria, and Silesia soon fell into his hands, the imperial chancellor, von Sinzendorff, who had so often opposed Eugene's counsels, is said to have declared, in his anxiety, "If Eugene were only alive we should know what to do!" Of course, no one can tell whether Eugene would have had better success if he had been opposed to Frederick, but it is certain that Austria could not produce a second Eugene from among her many warriors and statesmen. He remained "the only," "the great Eugene."

The last campaigns against the French (1734-1735) had shattered his already much impaired health. He was troubled with a bad cough, so that for days together he was not able to speak a word. Then a short period of relief would come, so that he could attend to public and private business or spend an hour with some old friend. One of his favorite recreations was to visit the venerable and gifted Hungarian Countess Batthiany of an evening for a game of piquet. His closed carriage passed slowly through the streets, and the horses are said to have known the house and to have stopped there of their own accord. But very likely no one would get out, for the master, the coachman, and the servant were all napping. Each one had then to be aroused separately, which no doubt caused a great deal of merriment each time. He had become very old and tired. The hardships of war had greatly weakened him, and the eighteen wounds which he had received in fourteen great battles and countless skirmishes also counted against him. He had passed the limit which the sacred book sets to human life.

On the twentieth of April, 1736, he had had his game of cards as usual in the society of the Countess Batthiany, but had been exceptionally quiet. On his arrival at home he complained that breathing was difficult, but refused to see a doctor and went to bed! About midnight, when his faithful old servant went in once more to look after his beloved master, he found him sleeping quietly, and softly withdrew. The next morning the servant noticed that his master was sleeping unusually late, also that he had not heard him cough. So he opened the door and approached the Prince's bed. He was dead; a congestion of the lungs had quietly ended his active and useful life.

When the news of the Prince's demise became known in Vienna, it produced general dismay and deep mourning. No one was more deeply grieved than the Emperor. He gave orders for a funeral such as no Austrian subject had ever had before, to honor the hero. "It shall serve to show," said the Emperor, "that the services of the departed shall never be forgotten by me."

Almost the whole population of Vienna flocked to see the Prince as he lay in state. Fourteen Field-Marshals were the pall-bearers, and the grateful Emperor himself attended the funeral services in the Cathedral of Saint Stephen. The eloquent Father Peickart preached the sermon on the text: "And departing, he has left us an example in his death which should be an inspiration to virtue, for the young as well as the old."

Footnotes

[1] Formerly one of the titles of the King of France.

[2] Since the powerful emperor of united Germany keeps guard upon the Rhine, France may no longer forbid any of our countrymen her dominions.

[3] Budapest is the official name of Buda and Pest, or Pesth. It is the capital of Hungary. Buda is on the west bank of the Danube and Pest on the east. The German name of Buda is Ofen.

[4] "The regiments were so destitute of accoutrements that the officers were ashamed of commanding them. If a troop was sent three or four miles away, at least half of the men were left fainting by the roadside. The starved men looked more like shadows than human beings."—Thus wrote Eugene to the Emperor.

Milton Keynes UK
Ingram Content Group UK Ltd.
UKHW030720041024
449263UK00004B/357